United States
Department of
Agriculture

**Forest
Service**

**North Central
Research Station**

**General Technical
Report NC-258**

Soils as an Indicator of Forest Health: A Guide to the Collection, Analysis, and Interpretation of Soil Indicator Data in the Forest Inventory and Analysis Program

I0410903

Katherine P. O'Neill, Michael C. Amacher, and Charles H. Perry

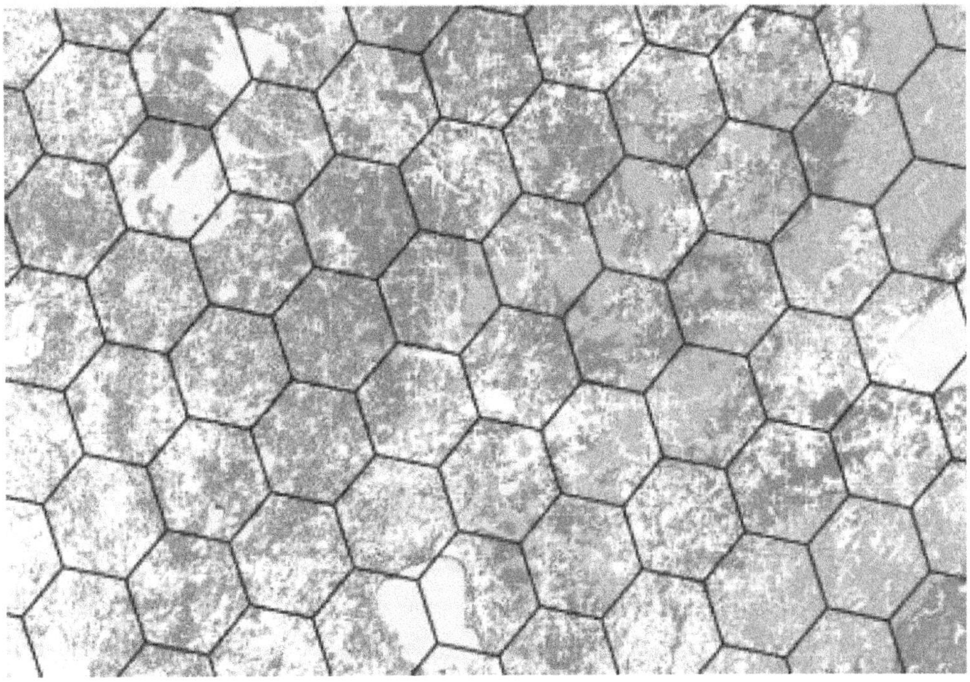

Abstract

The Montreal Process was formed in 1994 to develop an internationally agreed upon set of criteria and indicators for the conservation and sustainable management of temperate and boreal forests. In response to this effort, the Forest Inventory and Analysis (FIA) and Forest Health Monitoring (FHM) programs of the USDA Forest Service have implemented a national soil monitoring program to address specific questions related to: (1) the current and future status of soil resources and (2) the contribution of forest soils to the global carbon cycle. As the first and only nationally consistent effort to monitor forest soil quality in the United States, this program provides critical baseline information on the current status of the soil resource and the potential effects of natural and human disturbance on forest health and productivity.

This report provides documentation on the types of data collected as part of the FIA soil indicator, the field and laboratory methods employed, and the rationale behind these data collection procedures. Particular emphasis is placed upon describing generalized approaches for analyzing and interpreting soil indicator variables and discussing the strengths and limitations of individual soil variables. The analytical techniques detailed in this report are not intended to be exhaustive. Details of specific analytical approaches will be provided in a series of subsequent publications. Rather, the purpose of this report is to provide guidance to analysts and researchers on ways to incorporate soil indicator data into reports and research studies.

O'Neill, Katherine P.; Amacher, Michael C.; Perry, Charles H.

2005. Soils as an indicator of forest health: a guide to the collection, analysis, and interpretation of soil indicator data in the Forest Inventory and Analysis program. Gen. Tech. Rep. NC-258. St. Paul, MN: U.S. Department of Agriculture, Forest Service, North Central Research Station. 53 p.

Documents the types of data collected as part of the Forest Inventory and Analysis soil indicator, the field and laboratory methods used, and the rationale behind these data collection procedures. Guides analysts and researchers on incorporating soil indicator data into reports and research studies.

KEY WORDS:
Forest inventory, FIA, soils, forest health monitoring, sampling, estimation, analysis, reporting.

Acknowledgments

The soil indicator program began in the early 1990s and has benefited from the efforts and direction of numerous investigators since then. The original pilot studies were led by Mike Papp and Rick Van Remortel at the U.S. Environmental Protection Agency. Berman Hudson (USDA Natural Resources Conservation Service) continued the development of Forest Health Monitoring soil protocols from 1994 to 1996. Craig Palmer (University of Nevada-Las Vegas) served as the Forest Health Monitoring lead for this indicator from 1995 until 2000 and was responsible for developing and implementing many of the protocols described in this document.

Before 2000, laboratory analysis of soil samples was directed by Russ Dresbach and R. David Hammer at the University of Missouri Soil Characterization Lab. In 2001, three laboratories were added to the program: (1) the North Central Forestry Sciences Laboratory in Grand Rapids, Minnesota, previously managed by Don Nagel and William Pettit; (2) the Rocky Mountain Forestry Sciences Laboratory in Logan, Utah, directed by Mike Amacher; and (3) the International Institute of Tropical Forestry directed by Mary Jeanne Sanchez.

In addition, of vital importance to the soil monitoring program are the State forest health coordinators, regional trainers, field crews, quality assurance staff, and laboratory technicians who collect, verify, and analyze the soil data. Without their efforts and commitment to data quality, the soil monitoring program would not be possible.

Table of Contents

Table of Contents *continued*

Soils as an Indicator of Forest Health: A Guide to the Collection, Analysis, and Interpretation of Soil Indicator Data in the Forest Inventory and Analysis Program

1. INTRODUCTION

Because of the long association between soil science and agriculture, the term "soil health" has traditionally been associated solely with the capacity of the soil to promote plant growth. Renewed interest in principles of sustainable management has expanded this definition to recognize the broader role that soils play in regulating key ecosystem functions such as protecting watersheds through regulation of infiltration and runoff, preventing and mitigating pollution inputs, and providing physical support as a foundation material for roads and other development (Lal *et al.* 1997). In response to the need for more detailed information about changes in the status of forest soils, the USDA Forest Service has implemented a national monitoring program as part of its Forest Inventory and Analysis (FIA) plot network to address specific questions related to the long-term sustainability of our Nation's soil and water resources.

The purpose of this report is to present an overview of the current stage of development of this soil monitoring program and to provide guidance to analysts, researchers, and managers interested in using FIA soil data to address questions related to conservation and sustainable forest management. The discussion is divided into sections addressing the three primary foci of the soil indicator: soil compaction, soil erosion, and soil physical and chemical properties. For each topic, detailed information is provided regarding the types of data collected by FIA, the monitoring questions that these measurements were designed to address, and the importance of these measurements to the assessment of forest health. Field and laboratory methods are described for each measured variable along with a discussion of the strengths and potential limitations of these approaches. Finally, this report provides examples of analytical techniques that may be used to interpret these variables and to link soil measurements to ancillary data sets and models.

1.1 Indicators of Conservation and Sustainable Management

Regional and national monitoring of ecosystem function is a new and developing field of inquiry. Implementing and analyzing data from these large-scale monitoring programs requires field and analytical techniques that may differ from those typically applied in basic research or other technical fields. One of the underlying concepts in Forest Health Monitoring (FHM) is the use of "indicator" variables to assess change over time. Indicators are qualitative or quantitative variables that function as signals to relay complex ecological information in a simple and useful manner (Kurtz *et al.* 2001). To be effective, indicator variables must be indicative of a larger ecological process, easily measured, cost-effective, and repeatable (Burger and Kelting 1999). The large number of operational requirements necessary to make an indicator variable a useful monitoring tool limits the level of the detail that can be obtained. Taken in and of themselves, indicators cannot fully explain the causes for the observed changes or predict the future effects on ecosystem function. Once a trend has been identified during monitoring, indicator data must be evaluated in association with other monitoring data and targeted research to assess the potential impact on ecosystem function.

Because indicator variables are functionally defined, comparison of data over time and between different collection agencies requires

ABOUT THE AUTHORS

Katherine O'Neill[1] was formerly a Research Soil Scientist with the Forest Inventory and Analysis unit at the North Central Research Station in St. Paul, MN. She holds a B.S. in geology from the College of William and Mary and a Ph.D. in biogeochemistry and ecosystem ecology from Duke University. She joined the North Central Research Station in 2001 where she focused on the effects of disturbance on soil carbon and nutrient cycling and on the development of techniques for monitoring changes in forest soil properties. She also served as the soil indicator advisor for the eastern U.S. within the Forest Inventory and Analysis program from 2001 to 2003.

Michael Amacher is a Research Soil Scientist with the Reclamation of Disturbed Lands unit at the Forestry Sciences Laboratory in Logan, UT. He holds a B.S. and an M.S. in chemistry and a Ph.D. in soil chemistry, all from The Pennsylvania State University. He joined the Rocky Mountain Research Station in 1989. He studies the effects of natural and human-caused disturbances on soil properties and develops methods for restoring disturbed ecosystems. He is the western soil indicator advisor for FIA.

Charles H. (Hobie) Perry is a Research Soil Scientist with the Forest Inventory and Analysis unit at the North Central Research Station in St. Paul, MN. He holds a B.A. in philosophy from the University of Michigan and an M.S. and a Ph.D. in forestry from the University of Minnesota. He was on the faculty of Humboldt State University for 5 years and joined the NCRS in 2004. His current research focuses on estimation of the soils component of carbon stocks and methods of generalizing and summarizing FIA data across varying spatial scales. He is the eastern soil indicator advisor for FIA.

[1] Current affiliation: USDA Agricultural Research Service, Appalachian Farming Systems Research Center, Beaver, WV 25813.

consistency in applying and interpreting these definitions. The Montreal Process was formed in 1994 to develop an internationally agreed upon set of criteria and indicators for the conservation and sustainable management of temperate and boreal forests (Anonymous 1995). At a meeting of this working group in 1995, the participants reached consensus on seven criteria (table 1).

For each of these criteria, the working group established specific indicator variables that would be monitored to quantify the criteria. In the United States, a number of the indicator variables were already measured as part of national or regional monitoring efforts (e.g., FIA, National Water Quality Assessment Program, National Atmospheric Deposition Program). However, quantification of other indicator variables, such as those related to the conservation of soil resources (table 2), required the development of new monitoring initiatives. Together, the FIA, FHM, and Forest Health Protection (FHP) programs currently collect data that can be used to address more than half of the 67 Montreal Process indicators.

1.2 History of the Soil Indicator Program

FIA has served as the Nation's primary source of information on forest resources for more than 70 years. Over the past two decades, the FIA program has responded to evolving customer concerns and research needs by expanding its core inventory program to address a broader perspective on integrated resource management and sustainable

management and to monitor all forest lands regardless of ownership (Miles 2002, Stolte *et al.* 2002). During this same period, increasing concerns about forest health led State and Federal agencies to establish FHM, a cooperative effort to monitor and report on the long-term status, changes, and trends in U.S. forests. Beginning in the early 1990s, FHM developed, tested, and implemented a suite of monitoring variables that were closely related to indicator variables proposed by the Montreal Process: crown condition, ozone bioindicator species, lichen abundance and diversity, vegetation structure and diversity, down woody materials, and soil properties. Forest health indicators were developed with support from the scientific research community and represent a cooperative effort between university, State, and Federal investigators.

The Agricultural Research, Extension, and Education Reform Act (PL 105-185) of 1998 authorized transferring the Detection Monitoring portion of FHM plots to the Forest Inventory and Analysis program beginning with the 2001 field season. This integration provides a mechanism for repeated, systematic sampling of forest health indicators using nationally standardized collection, preparation, and data distribution formats that are compatible with forest inventory (McRoberts *et al.* 2004). Additional references documenting the merger of these two plot networks and the implications for statistical analyses may be found at the FIA library (available online at http://fia.fs.fed.us/library).

Table 1.—*Montreal Process criteria*

Criterion	Description
1	Conservation of biological diversity
2	Maintenance of productive capacity of forest ecosystems
3	Maintenance of forest ecosystem health and vitality
4	Conservation of soil and water resources
5	Maintenance of forest contributions to global carbon cycles
6	Maintenance and enhancement of long-term multiple socio-economic benefits to meet the needs of societies
7	Legal, institutional, and economic framework for forest conservation and sustainable management

Table 2.—*Indicators relating to the conservation of soil and water resources (Criterion 4) of the Montreal Process*

Indicator	Description
18	Area and percent of forest land with significant soil erosion
19	Area and percent of forest land managed primarily for protective functions (e.g., watersheds, flood protection, avalanche protection, riparian zones)
20	Percent of stream kilometers in forested catchments in which stream flow and timing has significantly deviated from the historic range of variation
21	Area and percent of forest land with significantly diminished soil organic matter and/or changes in other soil chemical properties
22	Area and percent of forest land with significant compaction or change in soil physical properties resulting from human activities
23	Percent of water bodies in forest areas with significant variance of biological diversity from the historic range of variability
24	Percent of water bodies in forest areas with significant variation from the historic range of variability in pH, dissolved oxygen, levels of chemicals (electrical conductivity), sedimentation, or temperature change
25	Area and percent of forest land experiencing an accumulation of persistent toxic substances

2. SAMPLING DESIGN

The joint FIA and FHM sampling design is derived from a systematic array of hexagons superimposed across the United States. Locations of permanent plots were randomly selected within each hexagon, and the entire plot array is considered an equal probability sample of the total surface area of the Nation. Each hexagon represents approximately 2,428 ha and is systematically assigned to one of five interpenetrating, non-overlapping panels (Brand et al. 2000). Panels are measured on a rotating basis with targets of one panel per year in the Eastern U.S. and one 50-percent subpanel per year in the Western U.S. (McRoberts et al. 2004). This design is derived from a global framework developed by the U.S. Environmental Protection Agency (USEPA) as part of the Environmental Monitoring and Assessment Program (EMAP) (Overton et al. 1990, USEPA 1997, White et al. 1992) and later implemented by FHM.

The FIA program consists of three phases (figs. 1 and 2). In Phase 1, land area is stratified using aerial photography or classified satellite imagery to increase the precision of estimates using stratified estimation. This process entails assigning each plot to a single stratum and determining the proportion of the land area represented by each stratum. In Phase 1, remotely sensed data may also be used to determine if plot locations have accessible forest land cover. In Phase 2, field crews visit plot locations that have accessible forest land cover, and they collect data on more than 300 variables, including land ownership, forest type, tree species, tree size, tree condition, and other site attributes (e.g., slope, aspect, disturbance, land use) (Smith 2002). Plot intensity for Phase 2 measurements is approximately one plot for every 2,428 ha of forested land (125,000 plots nationally).

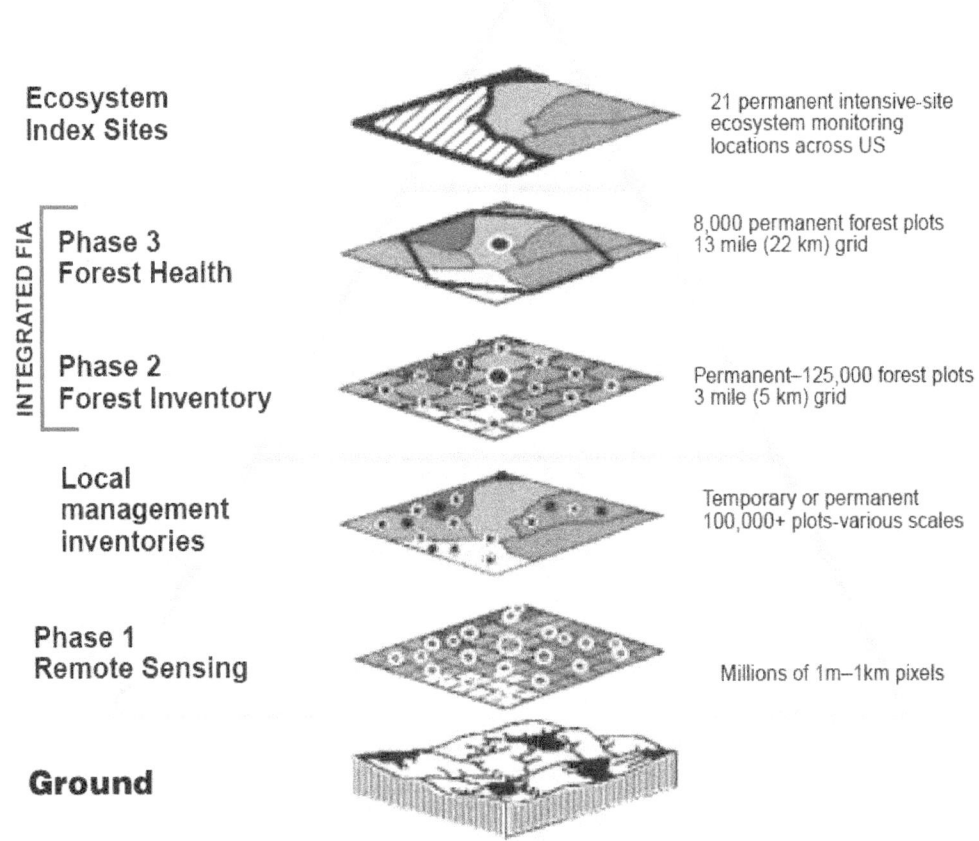

Ecosystem Index Sites — 21 permanent intensive-site ecosystem monitoring locations across US

INTEGRATED FIA

Phase 3 Forest Health — 8,000 permanent forest plots 13 mile (22 km) grid

Phase 2 Forest Inventory — Permanent–125,000 forest plots 3 mile (5 km) grid

Local management inventories — Temporary or permanent 100,000+ plots-various scales

Phase 1 Remote Sensing — Millions of 1m–1km pixels

Ground

Figure 1.—A schematic outline of the three-phase FIA sampling design. [Diagram from the FIA fact sheet series (available online: http://fia.fs.fed.us/library).]

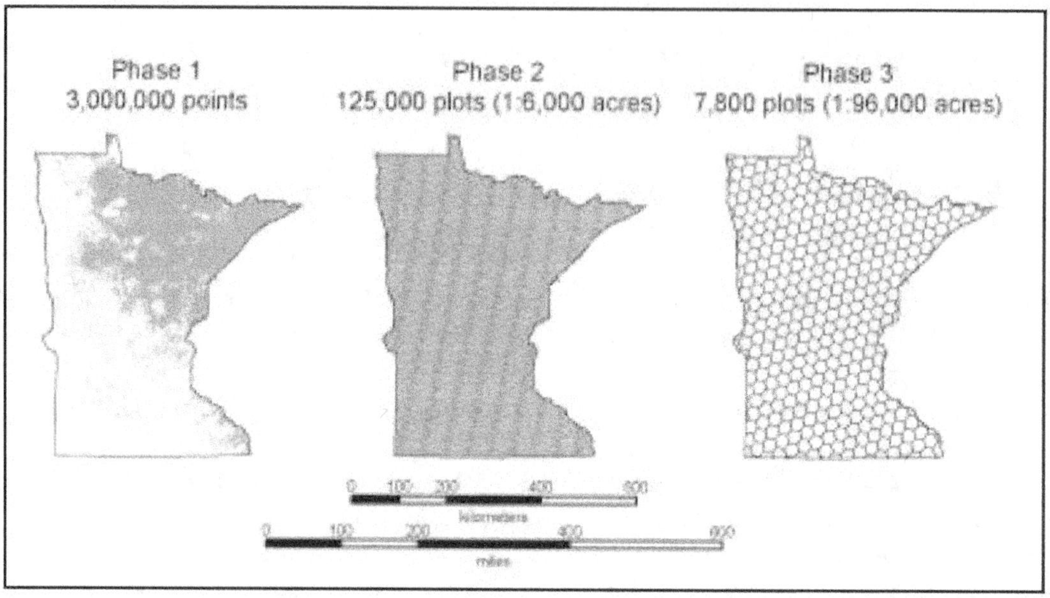

Figure 2.—An example of the three-phase FIA sampling design as implemented in Minnesota.

Phase 3 plots represent a 1:16 subset of Phase 2 sample plots (1 plot per 38,450 ha of forest land) that are measured for a broader suite of forest health attributes including tree crown conditions, lichen community composition, vegetation diversity and structure, down woody materials, and soil attributes. Phase 3 plots are assigned to one of five interpenetrating panels and are sampled once every 5 years. Data collection and analysis on Phase 3 plots is administered cooperatively by FIA, FHM, the FHP, State natural resource agencies, and universities. Because each Phase 3 plot is also a Phase 2 plot, all forest mensuration and ownership survey data are collected in concert with forest health data. As of the 2003 field season, soil monitoring had been implemented in 45 States and Puerto Rico. When the program is fully implemented, soil variables will be collected on approximately 7,800 plots measured over a 5-year cycle. Comprehensive reviews of the FIA sampling strategy may be found in Brand *et al.* (2000) and McRoberts *et al.* (2004).

Each FIA plot represents a circular sampling area of 1 ha and consists of a cluster of four 7.32-m- (1/60-ha-) radius subplots arranged in a triangular pattern around a central subplot (fig. 3). Subplot centers are located 36.6 m (120 ft) apart with the centers of subplots 2, 3, and 4 oriented at 120° angles around the plot center. The plot configuration includes smaller components for

sampling other forest attributes such as small trees, nonwoody vegetation, down woody debris, and vegetation diversity and structure. Each subplot is surrounded by a 17.95-m- (58.9-ft-) radius annular plot that is used for destructive sampling, including the collection of soil samples for chemical analysis. Plots are arranged in a fixed pattern regardless of the conditions (e.g., forest, grassland, road) on the plot.

Because of the interrelationship between the FIA and FHM programs, the soil monitoring program should also be considered as one part of a multitiered approach in FHM for assessing the ecological significance of changes in soil properties across the landscape. FHM consists of five interrelated and complementary activities: Detection Monitoring, Evaluation Monitoring, Intensive Site Monitoring, Research on Monitoring Techniques, and Analysis and Reporting (Tkacz 2003). Detection monitoring consists of nationally standardized aerial and ground surveys designed to collect baseline information on the current condition of forest ecosystems and to detect changes from those baselines over time. The ground survey portion of the FHM Detection Monitoring program is also now Phase 3 in FIA. Once a potential forest health concern has been identified on Detection Monitoring/Phase 3 plots, Evaluation Monitoring studies are used to examine the extent, severity, and probable causes of these changes. Intensive

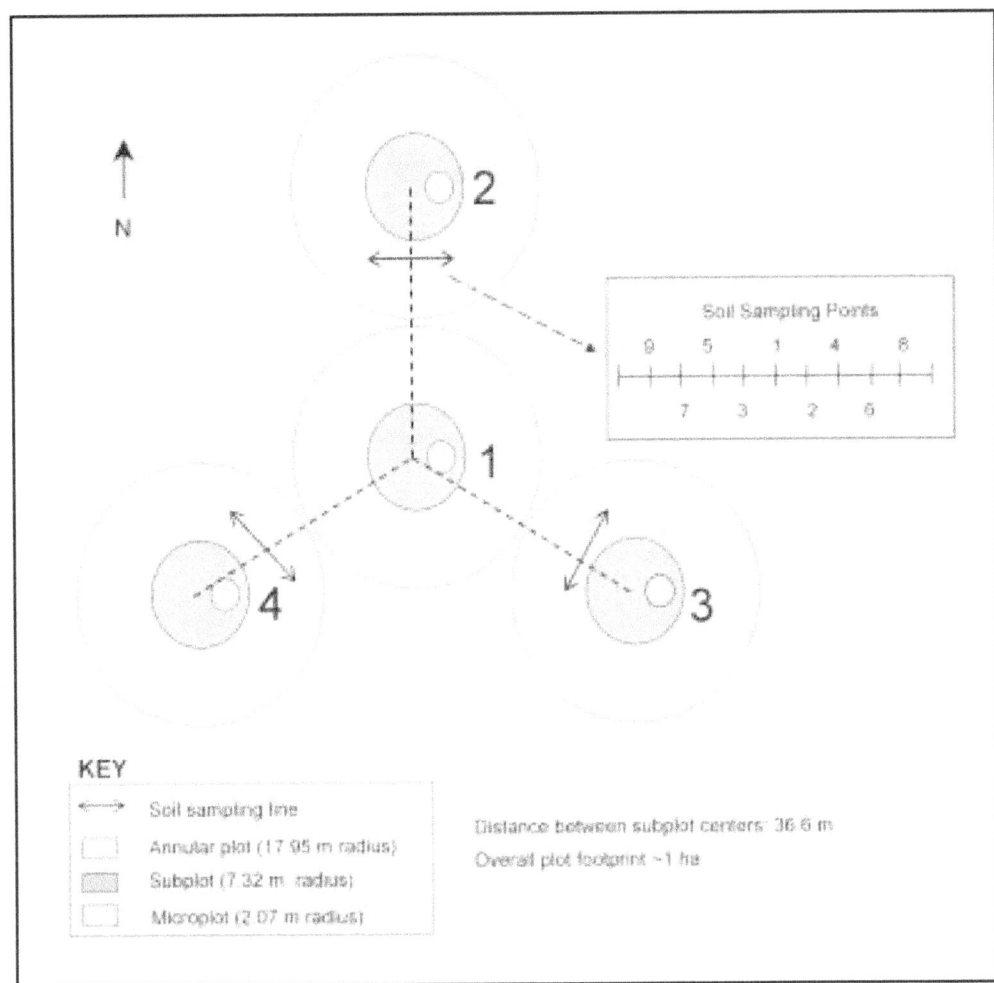

Figure 3.—Diagram of an FIA Phase 3 plot showing soil measurement locations. [Erosion and compaction are measured on the 7.32-m- (24-ft-) radius subplot. Soil samples are collected along soil sampling lines that run at a tangent to subplots 2, 3, and 4. During the first visit to a plot, field crews collect soils at point 1. Subsequent samples are spaced at 3-m (10-ft) intervals alternating on opposite sides of starting point 1.]

Site Monitoring projects are conducted to increase understanding of cause and effect relationships and assess specific issues at multiple spatial scales. Finally, Research on Monitoring Techniques focuses on developing and refining measurements to improve the efficiency and reliability of data collection and analysis.

3. COMPACTION

The FIA Phase 3 soil compaction measurements were developed to address Criterion 4, Indicator 22 from the Montreal Process: area and percent of forest land with significant compaction or change in soil physical properties resulting from human activities.

3.1 Rationale

Although soils are typically considered in terms of their mineral fractions, the term "soil" actually refers to a multiphase matrix of minerals, organic matter, water, and air. The ratio between these components largely determines the ability of the soil to support plant life. For optimal plant growth, about 50 percent of the total soil volume should consist of pore space that is equally filled with air and water (Fisher and Binkley 2000). Soil compaction occurs when the mineral portion of the soil becomes compressed by heavy equipment or by repeated passes of light equipment, people, or animals, thus reducing pore space and decreasing the volume of air in the soil. Under severe compaction, soil aggregates may break down entirely, resulting in "puddling" or the loss of soil structure by particles being dispersed in water and then settling to form a dense crust.

Compaction can have a variety of negative effects on soil fertility resulting from changes in both physical and chemical properties. Reduction in pore space makes the soil more dense and difficult to penetrate and can constrain the size, reach, and extent of root systems. In severe cases, this reduced rooting volume can lead to structural failure of the plant support system and destabilization of the entire tree. Reduction in soil aeration and water movement can reduce the ability of roots to absorb water, nutrients, and oxygen, resulting in shallow rooting and stunted tree forms. At the landscape scale, destruction of soil structure can limit water infiltration sufficiently to increase rates of runoff and soil loss from erosion. In addition to changes in soil physical properties, compaction can also significantly impact biological and chemical processes occurring in the soil. By reducing the oxygen content of the soil below that required for adequate respiration, severe compaction can disrupt root metabolism and move the soil towards an anaerobic condition.

3.2 Variables Used to Assess Compaction

Variables used to assess soil compaction are measured on all four of the FIA subplots (fig. 3). These measurements are based primarily on visual assessments of compacted areas and crew assessments of the type of compaction associated with compacted areas.

3.2.1 Percent compacted area

Field crews record a two-digit code indicating the percentage of the subplot that exhibits evidence of compaction (table 3). Soil compaction is assessed relative to the conditions of adjacent undisturbed soil. Improved roads are not included in this evaluation.

To quantify compacted areas, crews are trained to identify five different "evidences" of compaction: (1) increased soil density; (2) platy soil structure; (3) impressions or ruts in the soil (at least 5 cm into the mineral soil); (4) loss of soil structure (e.g., puddling); and, (5) mottling (specks of orange and/or green indicating a recent change in soil aeration). For evidences that require excavation, compacted soils are assessed relative to undisturbed soils off of the subplot to minimize plot disturbance. Before 2002, crews recorded the presence or absence of these evidences as part of the compaction data. In 2002, these variables were dropped from the indicator because they were not quantitative and data from the subplots could not be aggregated to the plot level.

Compaction is evaluated only for forested portions of the subplot. If the subplot includes nonforested areas, crews multiply the percentage of compaction on the forested part of the subplot by the fraction of the subplot that is in forested area. For example, if 50 percent of the subplot is forested and the compaction on the forested part is 30 percent, then compaction for the entire plot is 15 percent.

Table 3.—*Codes and cover classes used in assessing evidence of surface compaction*

Code	Surface compaction percent	Code	Surface compaction percent	Code	Surface compaction percent
00	Absent	35	31-35	75	71-75
01	Trace	40	36-40	80	76-80
05	1-5	45	41-45	85	81-85
10	6-10	50	46-50	90	86-90
15	11-15	55	51-55	95	91-95
20	16-20	60	56-60	99	96-100
25	21-25	65	61-65		
30	26-30	70	66-70		

3.2.2 Type of compaction

If crews report any compacted area on a subplot, they also record the types of compaction encountered. For each of the compaction types, a value of "1" is recorded if the type is present; a value of "0" is recorded if it is not (table 4).

3.2.3 Bulk density (see also section 5.3.3)

Bulk density is the weight of a unit volume of dry soil, typically expressed in units of grams per cubic centimeter ($g\ cm^{-3}$). Higher bulk density values indicate a lower volume of pore space available for air and water exchange. High bulk densities also impede root growth and penetration. Root growth is typically impaired at bulk densities greater than $1.6\ g\ cm^{-3}$ (Brady and Weil 1996). Because of their tendency to form aggregates, fine-textured soils such as clays and loams will tend to have lower bulk densities than coarse-textured soils (table 5). Mineral soils with a large fraction of rocks and coarse fragments (> 2 mm in diameter) will have higher bulk densities than soils without significant coarse fragment content. In contrast, organic matter tends to reduce bulk density. As a result of its high organic matter content, the forest floor, which is comprised of the decomposing litter layer and the decomposed humus layer, will nearly always have a lower bulk density than mineral soils. Details on procedures and calculations for bulk density may be found in section 5.3.3.

Table 4.—*Types of compaction recorded*

Code	Description
TyRutTr	Rutted trail. Ruts must be at least 5 cm (2 in.) deep into mineral soil or 15 cm (6 in.) deep from the undisturbed forest litter surface.
TyComTr	Compacted trail (usually the result of many passes of heavy machinery or vehicles).
TyComAr	Compacted area. Examples include the junction areas of skid trails, landing areas, heavily grazed soils, and work areas.
TyOther	Other. An explanation must be entered in the plot notes.

Table 5.—*Approximate bulk densities for a variety of soils and soil materials*[1]

Material	Approximate bulk density (g cm^{-3})
Organic soils	0.1-0.7
Pine wood	0.7
Forest loamy A horizons	0.7-1.2
Water	1.0
Cultivated clay and silt loams	0.9-1.6
Cultivated sandy loams and sands	1.2-1.8
Concrete	2.1
Compacted glacial till	1.9-2.2
Quartz mineral	2.65

[1]Adapted from Brady and Weil (1996).

3.3 Analysis and Interpretation

Data from the compaction indicator can be analyzed at the regional or national level. The compacted area reported for each subplot may be averaged to determine the mean compacted area per plot.

$$\overline{C} = \frac{\sum C_s}{n} \qquad (1)$$

where $\overline{C}$ is the mean compaction on the plot, C_s is the area of the subplot compacted, and n is the number of subplots. Because of the highly localized nature of soil compaction, attention should also be paid to plots on which two or more subplots show "significant" levels of compaction. Percent compacted area is recorded by cover class, and crews record a value of "01" to indicate trace levels of compacted soils. In practice, trace levels of surface soil compaction may occur during the course of plot measurements and are not usually indicative of a management effect.

Despite the importance of aeration and soil strength in regulating soil fertility, there are no widely accepted standards of what constitutes significant compaction. Compaction varies greatly in nature and depends on physical properties and the moisture content of the soil. As a result, the extent of soil compaction that should be considered ecologically significant will differ regionally depending on soil texture, forest cover, and landscape position.

Wherever possible, data from the compaction variables should be interpreted with respect to the texture and bulk density of samples collected from the same plot. Under comparable conditions, soils with a range of soil particle sizes (i.e.,

fine sandy loam) are generally more susceptible to compaction than soils with a more uniform particle size distribution. In these soils, disturbance causes the finer soil particles to fill the larger macropores formed by the coarse particle fraction, producing a denser soil. Although finely textured soils have more pore space and can hold more water per unit volume, the effects of compaction may be less permanent in these soils because of shrinking and swelling in response to wetting and drying. In general, the risk of compaction damage also tends to increase with increasing moisture content; the greatest sensitivity to compaction occurs at moisture contents that are near but below field capacity (the percentage of water remaining in a soil 2 or 3 days after it has been saturated and free drainage has ceased). This occurs because water reduces soil strength and acts as a lubricant between soil particles, increasing the degree of compaction following application of a load.

3.4 Examples of Analyses

To illustrate how soil erosion data may be used in FIA, FHM, or other reporting efforts, evidence of surface compaction and bulk density was evaluated for 227 plots in Minnesota, Wisconsin, and Michigan. During 1999 to 2000, the majority of plots (166 plots or 73.1 percent) reported no evidence of surface compaction (fig. 4). Only 25 of the 227 plots (11.0 percent) reported compaction on more than 10 percent of the plot area (fig. 4). The 10 plots reporting evidence of compaction on more than half of the plot were distributed across the three-State region and did not appear to correspond to a particular forest or soil type (fig. 5).

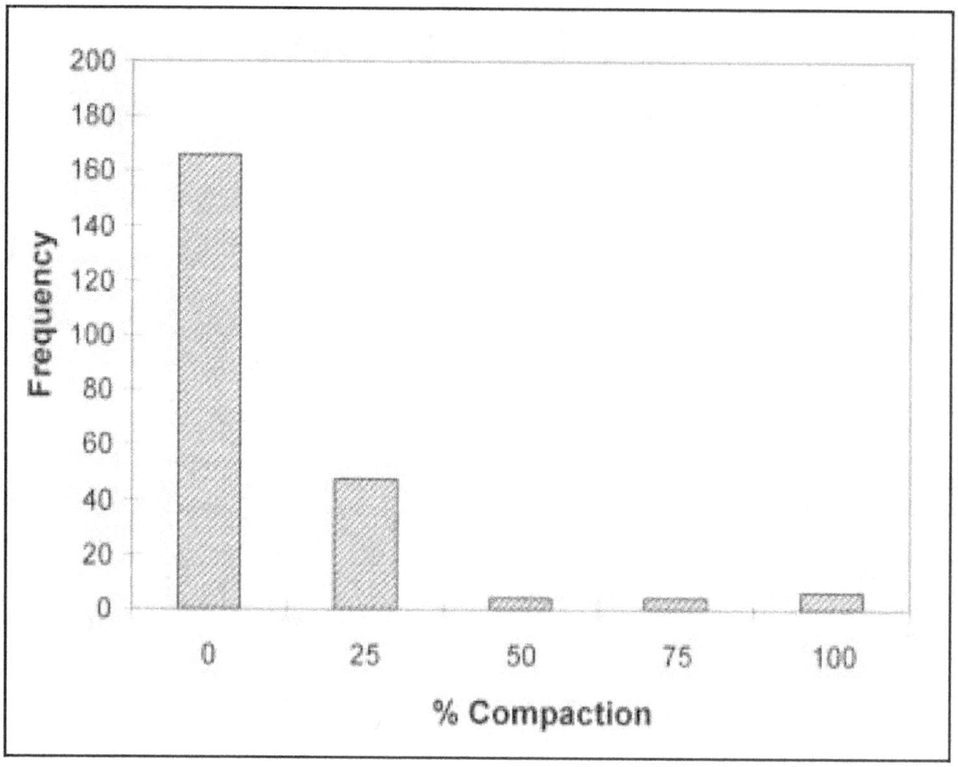

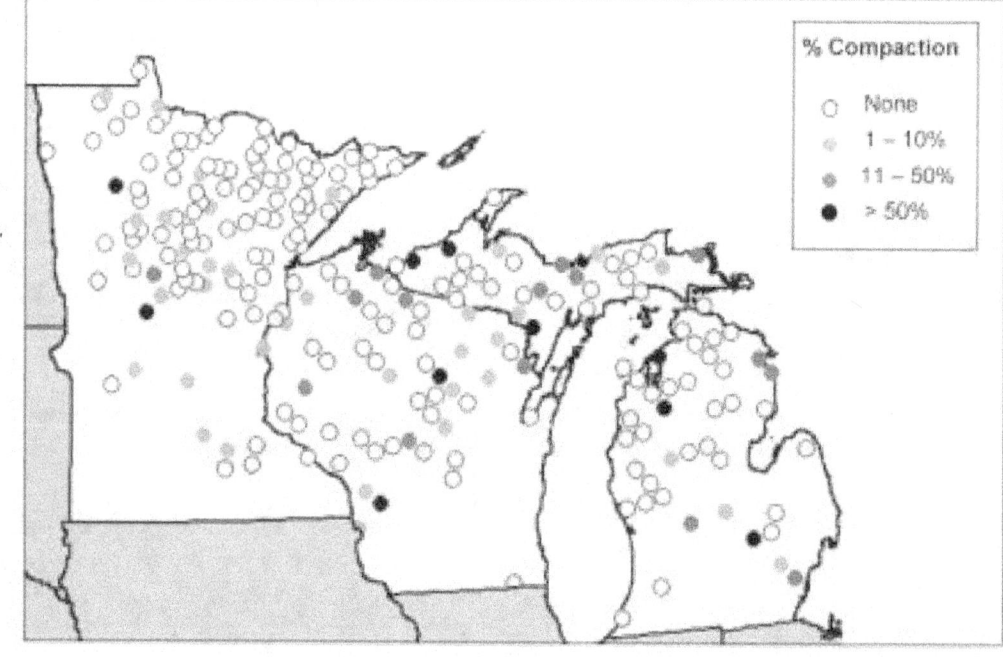

Figure 4.—Frequency distribution of soil compaction (surface disturbance) reported for plots measured in Minnesota, Michigan, and Wisconsin (1999-2000).

Figure 5.—Soil compaction reported for plots measured in Minnesota, Michigan, and Wisconsin (1999-2000). [Mean plot values were determined as the mean value from measurements made on the three subplots.]

From 2000 to 2002, the mean bulk density ± 1 standard deviation for the 0- to 10-cm soil layer was 1.01 ± 0.32 g cm^{-3} (n = 290) (fig. 6). Mean bulk densities measured for the 10- to 20-cm layer were higher at 1.36 ± 0.26 g cm^{-3} (n = 293; two-tailed t-test, P < 0.0001). Bulk density values were highly correlated with organic carbon (C) content for the 0- to 10-cm cores, suggesting that samples toward the lower end of the bulk density range may be a result of the incorporation of some O horizon materials due to crew error in identifying the break between the forest floor and mineral soil horizons (fig. 7). Only 2.8 percent of the 0- to 10-cm samples (8 out of 290 samples) had a measured bulk density greater than 1.5 g cm^{-3}, supporting the assessment that surface compaction was not widespread on the FIA plots measured.

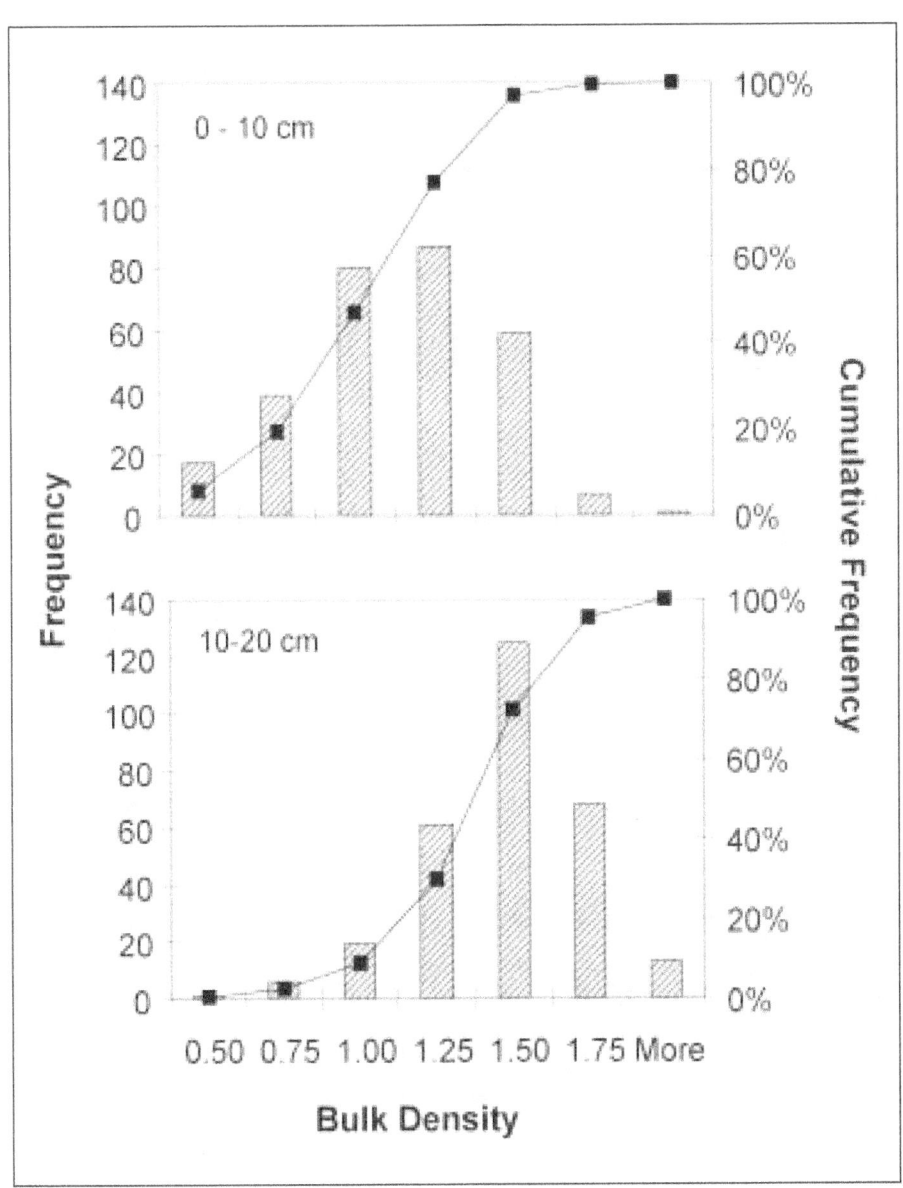

Figure 6.—Frequency distribution of bulk density values collected from 0- to 10-cm and 10- to 20-cm cores collected in Minnesota, Michigan, and Wisconsin (2000-2002).

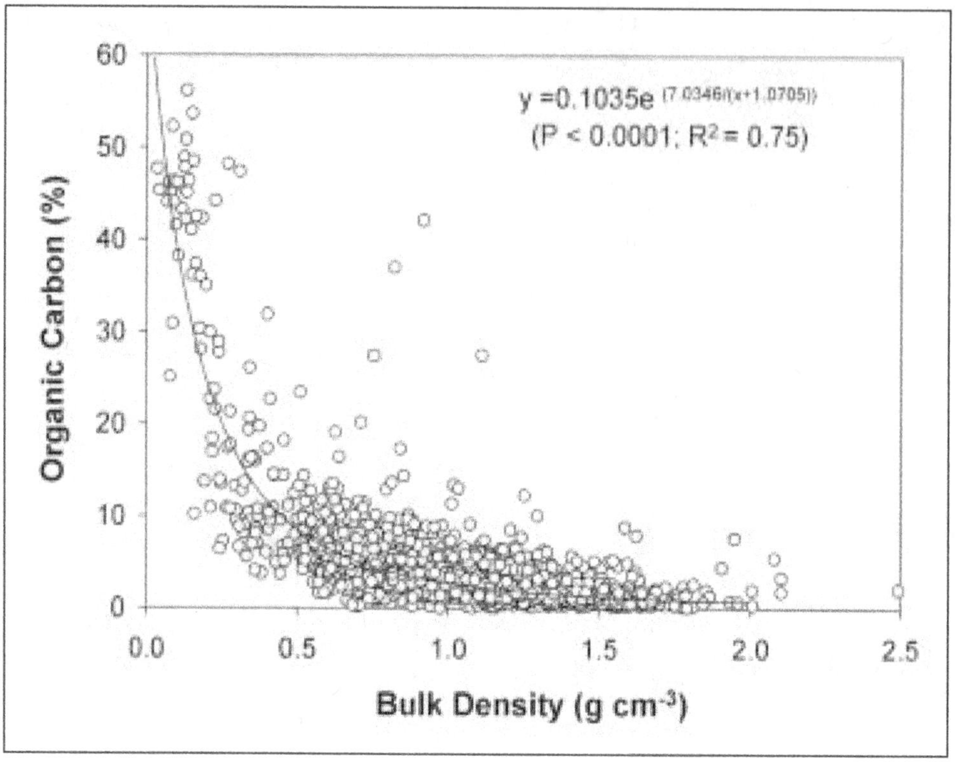

$$y = 0.1035e^{(7.0346/(x+1.0705))}$$
$$(P < 0.0001; R^2 = 0.75)$$

Figure 7.—Organic carbon content as a function of bulk density (0- to 10-cm cores) (O'Neill *et al.*, in press).

3.5 Limitations to Data

Soil physical properties are not conventionally monitored in a way that facilitates national reporting. Changes in soil bulk density in response to harvesting or other disturbances are usually measured on a site-specific basis. More quantitative measurements of compaction severity using techniques such as cone penetrometer or shear strength estimates are sensitive to variations in soil moisture content, complicating comparison of data collected on different sampling dates or in different regions. Current measurements of compaction on FIA plots are based primarily on visual estimates of compacted area. Subsurface compaction more than a few years old may not be readily visible to field crews and may be under-reported. In addition, measurements do not reflect the degree or intensity of compaction. Pilot studies are underway to develop additional, more quantitative, measures of soil compaction based on the use of pocket penetrometers (Amacher and O'Neill 2004).

4. EROSION

The FIA Phase 3 soil erosion measurements were developed to address Criterion 4, Indicator 18 from the Montreal Process: area and percent of forest land with significant soil erosion.

4.1 Rationale

Soil erosion is a natural geologic process in the building up and wearing down of the land surface. However, for resource managers concerned with optimizing production on a specific parcel of land, erosion can threaten soil, water, and related forest and plant resources. Extensive areas of soil erosion can have a major effect on aquatic ecosystems associated with forests, recreational opportunities, potable water supplies, and the lifespan of river infrastructure such as dams. By removing stored nutrients and organic matter from the soil surface, accelerated erosion also diminishes the capacity of the soil to support vegetation. On a global basis, the amount of nitrogen (N), phosphorus (P), and potassium (K) removed by erosion is estimated at more than 38 million Mg yr^{-1} (Brady and Weil 1996).

Although rates of erosion in undisturbed forest ecosystems tend to be low due to thick surface organic layers and tree roots that hold the soil in place, accelerated losses of surface soils can result from the removal of plant cover and the breakdown in root system integrity following site disturbance, harvest, and site preparation. High rates of localized soil erosion can also occur in response to the construction of roads on steep hillsides or to the harvesting of trees on sites with fragile or erodible soils. In addition, hydrophobic (water repellent) soils that result from wildfires are susceptible to erosion because water will tend to flow across the soil surface as runoff instead of infiltrating into the soil profile.

4.2 Variables Used to Assess Soil Erosion

Variables used to assess soil erosion are measured on all four of the FIA subplots (fig. 3). These measurements are based primarily on measurements of exposed bare soil, plant cover, soil texture, and slope. Plot data are then combined with ancillary information on climate and landscape position to parameterize soil erosion models.

4.2.1 Percent bare soil

On each subplot, field crews visually assess ground cover and record a two-digit code to indicate the percentage of the 7.31-m-radius subplot that is covered by bare soil (mineral or organic) (table 6). Fine gravel (2-5 mm) is considered part of the bare soil. However, large rocks protruding through the soil (e.g., bedrock outcrops) are not included in this category since these are not erodible surfaces. For the soil indicator, cryptobiotic crusts are not considered bare soil.

Percent bare soil is evaluated only for forested portions of the subplot. If the subplot includes nonforested areas, crews multiply the percentage of bare soil on the forested part of the subplot by the fraction of the subplot that is in forested

Table 6.—*Codes and cover classes used in evaluating percent bare soil*

Code	Bare soil percent	Code	Bare soil percent	Code	Bare soil percent
00	Absent	35	31-35	75	71-75
01	Trace	40	36-40	80	76-80
05	1-5	45	41-45	85	81-85
10	6-10	50	46-50	90	86-90
15	11-15	55	51-55	95	91-95
20	16-20	60	56-60	99	96-100
25	21-25	65	61-65		
30	26-30	70	66-70		

area. For example, if 50 percent of the subplot is forested and the coverage of bare soil on the forested part is 30 percent, then bare soil for the entire plot is 15 percent.

4.2.2 Soil texture

After collecting a sample core for chemical analysis (described in section 5.2), field crews assess the texture of soils in the 0- to 10-cm and 10- to 20-cm layers (table 7). Texture estimation is done in the field by hand texturing a moistened sample (approximately the consistency of modeling clay or wet newspaper) between the thumb and forefinger. The moistened sample is wet enough to saturate all of the particles but not so moist that excess water flows freely from the sample when squeezed. Soils that cannot form a ball and have a grainy texture are coded either as sandy or coarse sand. Soils that will form a ball and a self-supporting ribbon are coded as clayey. Soils that will form a ball but not a ribbon are coded as loamy.

Table 7.—*Codes used for recording soil texture*

Code	Description
0	Organic
1	Loamy
2	Clayey
3	Sandy
4	Coarse sand

4.2.3 Slope angle

Slope angle is measured as part of the Phase 2 data collection by sighting a clinometer along a line parallel to the average incline (or decline) of each subplot. This angle is measured along the shortest pathway downslope before the drainage direction changes. Data are recorded to the nearest 1 percent. In cases where the slope changes gradually across the subplot, the average slope is recorded. However, if the slope change is predominantly of one direction, crews code the predominant slope percentage rather than the average. Should the subplot fall directly on or straddle a canyon bottom or narrow ridgetop, crews code the average slope of the side hills (if subplot center falls directly in the center) or the slope of the side hill on which the majority of the plot falls.

4.2.4 Vegetation structure

Before 2002, percent vegetation cover (< 6 ft tall) was estimated for each 24-ft-radius subplot based on visual assessments. Detailed measurements of understory plant canopy height were then collected on three 4-ft-diameter erosion microplots established on each subplot. Details of this sampling design are provided in table 8. This sampling design was developed for use with specific tables in the Universal Soil Loss Equation (USLE) model (Renard *et al.* 1997, Wischmeier and Smith 1978).

With the addition of the vegetation diversity and down woody materials indicators to the FIA Phase 3 program, analysis of soil erosion models indicated that measurements on the soil erosion plots could be replaced with data collected by other indicators. On plots where all three indicators have been implemented, this restructuring has significantly reduced time for the field crews without a loss of analytical power. In particular, more detailed information on the cover and structure of understory vegetation may now be obtained from measurements collected as part of the vegetation diversity indicator, allowing for the use of a number of different erosion models. In cases where the vegetation diversity data are not collected on a plot, other variables within the soil indicator (e.g., bare soil cover, forest floor thickness) are sufficient to model erosion losses using the Water Erosion Prediction Project (WEPP) model.

4.2.5 Forest floor thickness

When collecting soil samples (section 5.2), field crews record the thickness of the forest floor measured from the top of the litter layer to the boundary between the forest floor and mineral soil. Measurements are made at the north, east, west, and south edges of a 12-inch-diameter circular sampling frame (for a total of four measurements). Where bare soil or bedrock material is exposed, a depth of "0" is recorded.

Forest floor thicknesses are collected from soil sampling sites adjacent to subplots 2, 3, and 4. Samples are collected if, and only if, the soil sampling sites are forested. Additional information on forest floor thickness is collected as part of the down woody materials indicator and can be combined with these soil data to improve estimates of mean values.

Table 8.—*Changes in field protocols, 1998-2001*

Year(s) of implementation	Method
Vegetation height	
1998–2000	Three 4-ft-diameter erosion miniplots established on each subplot centered 12 ft north, south, and west of the subplot center. If duff thickness < 5 cm, mean height to lowest overhanging vegetation estimated from miniplot.
2001	If duff < 5 cm in thickness, height measured to lowest overhanging vegetation at the center and N, S, E, and W edges of the erosion miniplot. Median value recorded.
2002–present	Variable dropped because it overlaps with measurements made as part of the vegetation diversity indicator.
Slope length	
1998–2001	Estimated from the center of each subplot to the break in slope.
2002–present	Variable dropped.
Depth to restrictive horizon	
1998–2000	Depth to restrictive layer measured within forest floor sampling area. Mean value recorded.
2001–present	Depth to restrictive horizon measured at center and N, S, E, and W edges of forest floor sampling area. Median value recorded.
Forest floor thickness	
1998–2000	On each erosion plot, crew recorded the median of five measurements of forest floor thickness.
2001–present	Variable dropped from the erosion plots because it overlaps with measurements made as part of the down woody materials and vegetation diversity indicators.
Ground cover	
1998–2001	Visual percent cover estimates of bare soil, litter, and vegetation cover (< 6 ft tall) on all subplots.
2002 - present	Visual percent cover estimates of bare soil on all subplots.

4.3 Models Used to Assess Erosion

Because of the expense and logistical difficulty of directly measuring erosion losses in the field, potential erosion losses are frequently estimated by using of empirical or functional models based on field data. FIA is currently evaluating two models for estimating soil erosion risk: USLE and WEPP. A complete description of these models is beyond the scope of this report. Parameterization of both of these erosion models will be documented in detail in a future set of publications (e.g., Amacher *et al.*, in review).

4.3.1 Universal Soil Loss Equation

USLE is an empirical model designed to predict the longtime average soil loss from runoff from specific field areas under specified cropping and management systems (Dissmeyer and Foster 1981, 1984; Renard *et al.* 1991; Wischmeier and Smith 1978). The USLE models sediment detachment as a function of five parameters, following:

$$A = RKLSCP$$

The definitions for these variables are provided in table 9. Some of these factors may be directly measured on FIA plots; others are determined from modeling or from ancillary data sets.

Each of these five parameters represents the numerical estimate of a specific condition that affects the severity of soil erosion at a particular location. However, the erosion values reflected by these factors can vary considerably under different weather conditions. Therefore, the values obtained from USLE more accurately represent long-term averages and cannot be applied to model losses from a specific year or storm. In addition, USLE does not account for soil losses from gully, wind, or tillage erosion.

USLE was designed for use in agricultural systems, and as such, applying the model to a forested landscape requires interpretation and additional research to develop consistent criteria for assigning these parameters. USDA Forest Service scientists are currently working with the Natural Resources Conservation Service to develop

Table 9.—*Erosion factors used in the USLE model*

Symbol	Factor	Description	Data source for modeling FIA plots
R	Climatic erosivity	Calculated from the annual summation of rainfall energy in every storm multiplied by its maximum 30-minute intensity.	Estimated
K	Soil erodibility	The average soil loss in tons acre^{-1} per unit area for a particular soil in cultivated, continuous fallow with an arbitrarily selected slope length of 72.6 ft and slope steepness of 9%.	Estimated
L	Slope length	A ratio of soil loss under given conditions to that at a site with the "standard" slope steepness of 9% and slope length of 72.6 ft.	Estimated
S	Slope gradient	See above	Measured
C	Cover and management	Reflects the effects of practices that reduce the quantity and rate of water runoff and thus reduce the amount of erosion.	Measured
P	Erosion control practice	The ratio of soil loss from land cropped under specified conditions to corresponding loss under tilled, continuous fallow conditions. Used to determine the relative effectiveness of soil and crop management systems in preventing soil loss.	Estimated

methods for assigning variables to field plot conditions. Detailed information about the USLE and its application to forested soils can be found in Wischmeier and Smith (1978) and Renard *et al.* (1991).

4.3.2 Water Erosion Prediction Project

WEPP is a process-oriented, continuous simulation, erosion prediction model developed by an interagency team of researchers from the U.S. Departments of Agriculture (Forest Service, Agricultural Research Service, and Natural Resources Conservation Service) and Interior (Bureau of Land Management and U.S. Geological Survey). The model is applicable to small watersheds and mimics the natural processes that are important in soil erosion. Processes addressed in the model structure include infiltration and runoff; soil detachment, transport, and deposition; and plant growth, senescence, and residue decomposition.

Researchers at the USDA Forest Service Forestry Sciences Laboratory in Moscow, ID, have developed an interface to the WEPP model that specifically addresses erosion prediction on forest lands. This interface provides results in a summary form as well as probability tables that estimate the likelihood of a given level of erosion occurring following a particular disturbance. The technical documentation for Disturbed WEPP (Elliot *et al.* 2000) provides additional information about the disturbed forest interface and the WEPP model.

An example of a WEPP input table and guidelines for inputting model parameters is shown in table 10. Because WEPP uses slightly different texture designations from those collected by FIA field crews, a texture conversion table that shows the WEPP soil textures that correspond to the textures used by FIA is provided in table 11.

4.4 Analysis and Interpretation

Although the field methods for the erosion variables are relatively straightforward, analysis of soil erosion data is perhaps the most computationally difficult type of analysis within the soil indicator. Because of inherent differences in soil types, landscape positions, and climatic conditions, data on soil erosion are challenging to summarize in a statistically meaningful way. For both the USLE and WEPP modeling approaches, mean erosion rates may be calculated for each FIA plot (table 12). Plot-level data may then be aggregated to the regional level for population estimation.

4.5 Examples of Analyses

To illustrate how soil erosion data may be used in FIA, FHM, or other reporting efforts, erosion rates of 177 plots sampled in Washington, Oregon, and California in 1999 were modeled using WEPP. For this analysis, all plots were modeled as if they were in an undisturbed forest. Under average precipitation events, the WEPP model predicted no erosion on 49 percent of the plots (87 out of 177). Only 7.9 percent of plots

Table 10.—*Example of a WEPP input table for an FIA Phase 3 plot*[1]

Location[2]	Paradise Dam				
Soil texture[3]	Loam				

Element[4]	Treatment[5]	Gradient[6]	Length[7]	Area[8]	Cover[9]
		(%)	(feet)	(acres)	(%)
		35			
Upper	20-year-old forest		112		99
		35			
				1.33	
		35			
Lower	20-year-old forest		112		99
		35			

[1] Modified from Amacher *et al.*, in review.
[2] Select from climate station database.
[3] Choose sandy loam, silt loam, clay loam, and loam.
[4] WEPP divides a hillslope into upper and lower areas or elements, but it can also be applied to portions of a hillslope (e.g., plot area).
[5] Choose a forest or disturbance type. Choices for forest type are 20-year-old forest (mature forest) or 5-year-old forest (young forest). Choices for disturbance type are low-severity fires, high-severity fires, or skid trails.
[6] Use the mean of the slopes for all four subplots in the WEPP input table.
[7] Divide the whole plot area into upper and lower elements of equal slope length.
[8] Corresponds to a rectangular area surrounding all four subplots.
[9] Soil cover = 100 - percent bare soil. Use mean for all four subplots.

Table 11.—*Soil texture conversion table for converting soil texture data collected by FIA field crews into soil texture classes required by WEPP*

Soil textures in FIA field guide	Soil textures in WEPP
Coarse sand	Sandy loam
Sand	Sandy loam
Loam	Loam
Clay	Clay loam

Table 12.—*Soil erosion data collected from Phase 3 plots and input data needed for the USLE and WEPP models*[1]

FIA field data	USLE inputs	Disturbed WEPP inputs
—	Rainfall erosivity factor (R)	Climate station data
Soil texture	Soil erodibility factor (K)	Soil texture
Percent bare soil	Cover factor (C)	Total soil cover
Slope angle and length	Slope factor (LS)	Slope angle and length
—	Cultural practice factor (P)	—
Forest condition class & ancillary data	—	Forest or disturbance type

[1] Adapted from Amacher *et al.*, in review.

had a predicted erosion rate of greater than 1.0 Mg ha[-1] (fig. 8). Under a more severe precipitation event (100-year storm), the amount of modeled soil erosion increased, and 46.3 percent of plots had a modeled erosion rate greater than 1 Mg ha[-1] (median 0.74 Mg ha[-1]). Although the potential for erosion is greater under more extreme climate events, these mean erosion losses are still lower than the estimated 6.9 Mg ha[-1] annually lost from U.S. croplands (U.S. Department of Agriculture 2000). (Note: for State or regional reports, analysts may wish to

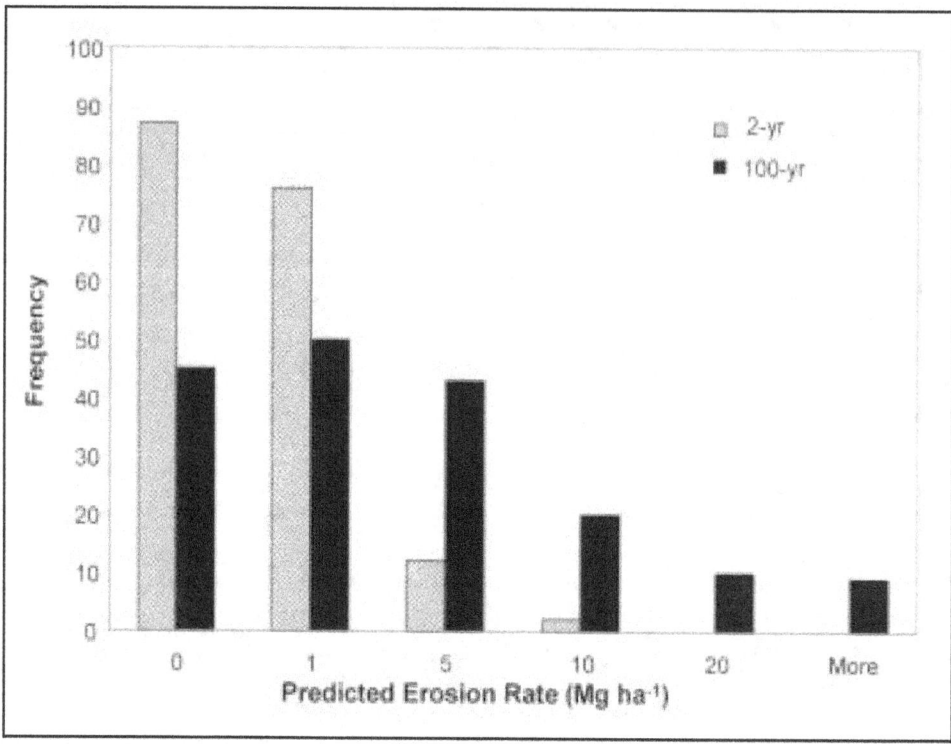

Figure 8.—Frequency distribution of WEPP-modeled erosion rates for plots in California, Oregon, and Washington (1999) under an average storm event (2-year return interval) and a 100-year storm event. [As an initial analysis, model runs assume an undisturbed forest.]

reference National Resources Inventory or Natural Resources Conservation Service data for that specific region; c.f. U.S. Department of Agriculture 2000.) Under severe weather events, the highest potential erosion rates were associated with plots on steep slopes located within the Coast Range in California, the foothills of the Sierra Nevada Mountains in California, and the Cascade Mountains in Washington and Oregon (fig. 9).

The majority of the factors used to model erosion rates (e.g., climate, soil texture, slope) are relatively static with regards to monitoring objectives. The primary management factor controlling changes in erosion losses from forested systems is the amount of bare soil exposed at the ground surface following disturbance (Conkling et al., in press; O'Neill and Amacher 2004). Data collected in 1999 indicate that, throughout the

Figure 9.—WEPP modeled erosion on FIA plots in California, Oregon, and Washington (1999) for two different storm intensities.

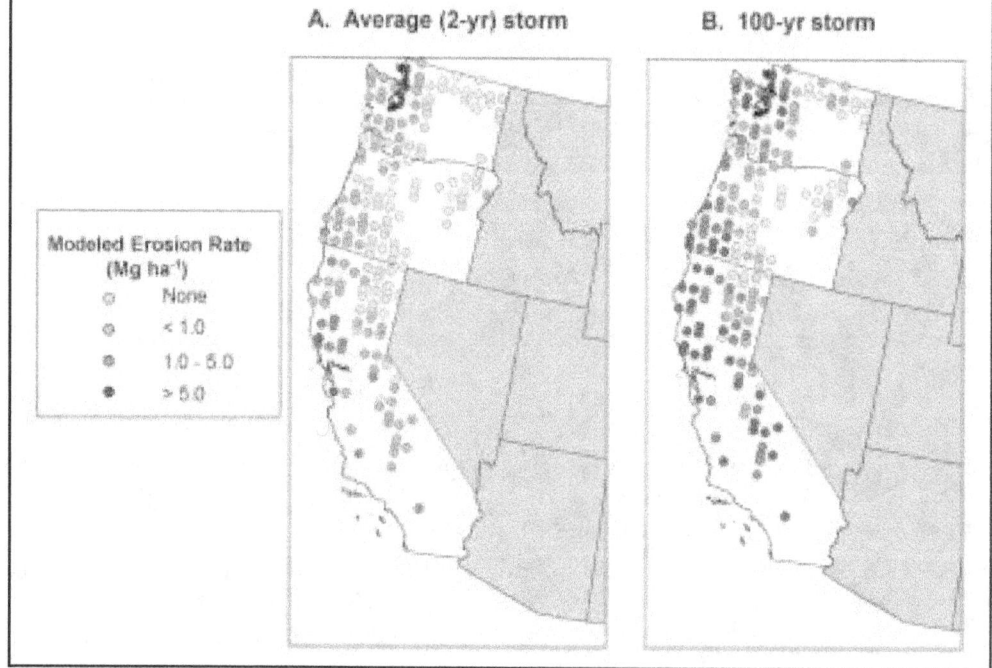

Pacific Northwest, the number of plots reporting levels of bare soil large enough to increase erosion estimates is relatively small. The majority of plots (57 percent) reported cover on more than 95 percent of the plot area (fig. 10). Less than 2 percent of plots (3 plots) measured in 1999 recorded areas of bare soil that covered more than half of the plot area.

Analysts should keep in mind that erosion estimates represent only modeled potentials under different rainfall intensities and do not reflect actual erosion losses. However, change in erosion rates, or a change in the distribution of plots exhibiting a high potential for erosion, may reflect trends in exposed ground cover, harvesting, or surface disturbance.

4.6 Data and Model Limitations

Because erosion estimates are made on the basis of modeled results, analysis of this indicator is necessarily limited by the assumptions of these models. It is also important to recognize that soils vary naturally in terms of their potential for soil erosion and their ability to tolerate these soil losses. For this reason, aggregate estimates of soil erosion have little meaning in and of themselves. Agricultural erosion monitoring programs typically measure soil erosion losses relative to the tolerable loss (T factor) for a given soil type. T factors are available from Natural Resources

Conservation Service soil survey maps and digital products such as the NRCS STATSGO (1:250,000) and SSURGO (1:12,000 to 1:63,360) databases. However, these tolerance values may not be directly applicable to forested soils, and additional research is needed to develop similar erosion loss terms for forested systems. Finally, even in regions where rates of erosion can be reliably estimated, the links between soil erosion and forest productivity are not always well understood.

4.6.1 USLE

USLE is an empirical model developed for use as a management tool for small tracts of land under agricultural management and was not designed for use in forested landscapes. As a result, USLE requires a number of assumptions that limit its usefulness in modeling soil erosion on forested lands. First, USLE calculates only an average soil erosion rate for a given precipitation and runoff factor based on long-term average climatic conditions. Second, the land practice factors in USLE were designed to represent agricultural management practices and, as such, parameterization of the model for common forest management practices is difficult and requires refinements to the published model parameters. Finally, USLE represents the first generation in a series of empirical models developed by the Natural Resources Conservation Service. Current

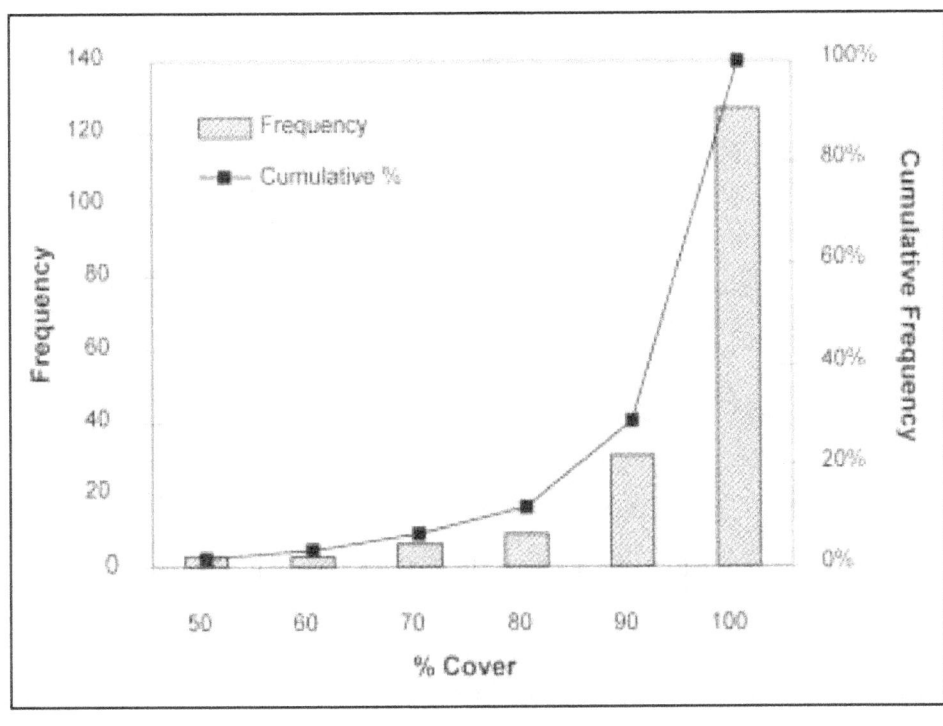

Figure 10.—Frequency distribution of mean soil cover on plots measured in California, Oregon, and Washington in 1999. [The value for each plot represents the pe cent of the plot covered by forest floor or other materials. Mean plot values were determined as the mean value from measurements made on the three subplots.]

estimates of erosion on agricultural lands are made using the Revised Universal Soil Loss Equation (RUSLE), which incorporates results from additional field experiments and other refinements to the original model (Foster *et al.* 1996). However, these refinements were not made to the woodland portion of the model, and estimates from forest lands must still be done using the earlier version. Additional research is needed to adapt the USLE model for use in FIA, and at present, modeled data should be reported as relative rather than as absolute values.

In addition to limitations of the model itself, there are analytical constraints associated with our current ability to apply USLE to FIA plots. Although soil erodibility (K) factors may be determined from soil texture measurements made in the field, these texture evaluations are only broken down into four general categories. In addition, the methods for slope length estimation (L) are currently being revised, and the availability of these data will be limited until the revised methods are reviewed and implemented.

An alternate approach for determining erodibility factors is to apply georeferenced data from digital soil surveys (e.g., the NRCS SSURGO databases). At present, digital county-level soil surveys are not available for all regions of the country. Use of digital products at coarser scales (NRCS STATSGO, 1:250,000) introduces a greater level of uncertainty and complexity into estimates because map units represent a composite of multiple soil components. As a result, there is no way to be certain that the mapped soil type reflects the actual conditions on the plot. Additional research is needed to develop standardized approaches for linking FIA plot data with soil survey data for use in automating erosion modeling.

4.6.2 WEPP

The WEPP model overcomes many of the limitations of USLE and provides a more realistic simulation of erosion processes operating on forested sites. First, instead of a single climate term based on long-term average values, WEPP uses climate data from a database of more than 2,600 weather stations to calculate precipitation, runoff, and soil erosion rates for episodic climate events of different return intervals (e.g., 100, 50, 20, 10, and 5 years). This direct linkage to long-term climate records makes it easy both to tabulate erosion rates for high, average, and low water years and quantify the potential effects of climatic extremes on soil erosion. Second, the databases contained within WEPP allow for soil erosion predictions under a variety of disturbance regimes such as fire and specific management practices. Third, fewer parameters are needed to initialize WEPP, and those parameters that are needed are easier to collect in the field. Forest Service scientists are currently working to develop techniques for modeling erosion from FIA plots using the WEPP model (Amacher *et al.*, in review).

5. SOIL PHYSICAL AND CHEMICAL PROPERTIES

The FIA Phase 3 soil chemistry measurements were developed in response to several indicators of the Montreal Process (table 13).

5.1 Rationale

The health and productivity of forest ecosystems may be adversely affected by changes in soil chemical or physical properties following disturbance or certain management practices. The goal of the soil chemical measurements is to quantify changes in soil properties relative to long-term average values that are sufficient to impact soil fertility and site productivity.

Soil organic matter (SOM) was selected as a key index of soil quality because of its importance as a regulator of soil chemical, biological, and physical properties. Forest ecosystems obtain most of their nutrients from the decomposition of litter, branches, and other organic materials near the soil surface. SOM contains a large number of exchange sites that increase the capacity of the soil to adsorb these nutrients and prevent them from leaching below the rooting zone. SOM can also adsorb potentially toxic levels of some elements (e.g., copper (Cu), cadium (Cd), aluminum (Al), lead (Pb)), thereby decreasing their bioavailability to microorganisms, plants, and animals. In addition to nutrient retention, SOM facilitates the transport of air and water through the soil by increasing moisture holding capacity and promoting the development of soil aggregates. Finally, SOM serves as a major reservoir for terrestrial C. On a global scale, soils are estimated to contain more C than the atmosphere itself (Schlesinger 1991). As concern grows about possible climatic responses to increased CO_2 emissions, an improved understanding of the capacity of forested systems to sequester C in soils is critical for developing national policy initiatives. Because SOM is concentrated at the soil surface, both its quantity and quality may change following certain forest operations and management practices.

Although SOM is a useful index variable for looking at trends across broad areas of the landscape, a more detailed evaluation of soil chemical and physical properties is necessary to address specific forest health and productivity concerns. For example, soil pH is a primary factor in determining the productivity of the soil through its regulation of soil nutrient availability, aggregate stability, and microbial activity. Maps of soil pH in relation to texture and forest type provide a baseline index of the weathering status and potential nutrient holding capacity of soils. Together with the concentrations of exchangeable sulfur (S), Al, and base cations such as sodium (Na), potassium (K), magnesium (Mg), and calcium (Ca), changes in soil pH over time provide a mechanism for monitoring the potential effects of soil acidification in response to industry and fossil fuel emissions. Concentrations of plant nutrients (N, P, K) may provide additional insight into questions about stand productivity, growth, and mortality. Finally, changes in concentrations of trace metals in the upper mineral soil may be used to monitor the effects of pollution and the accumulation of plant toxic substances in the soil.

Table 13.—*Montreal Process indicators addressed by soil chemistry measurements*

Indicator	Description
4.21	Area and percent of forest land with significantly diminished soil organic matter and/or changes in other soil chemical properties
4.25	Area and percent of forest land experiencing an accumulation of persistent toxic substances
5.27	Contribution of forest ecosystems to the total global carbon budget, including absorption and release of carbon

5.2 Methods

Soil chemical and physical properties are assessed through the collection of soil samples, which are then submitted to a regional laboratory for analysis. Samples of the forest floor and mineral soil are collected within the annular plot at pre-assigned locations along soil sampling lines adjacent to subplots 2, 3, and 4 (fig. 3). Initial sampling points are located 27.4 m (90 ft) from the plot center along the azimuth lines to the centers of subplots 2, 3, and 4. Subsequent remeasurement locations are spaced at 3-m (10-ft) intervals alternating on opposite sides of the initial sampling point. Soils are collected if, and only if, the pre-assigned soil sampling location is forested, regardless of the condition of the subplot. On plots where an obstruction (e.g., boulder, standing water) prevents collection at the designated sampling point, the sampling point may be relocated within a radius of 1.5 m (5 ft).

5.2.1 Forest floor

The forest floor is comprised of two layers. The upper layer of fresh or decomposing plant parts is referred to as the litter layer. The primary distinguishing characteristic of this layer is that plant parts are either undecomposed or are only partially decomposed but still recognizable. Twigs, deciduous tree leaves, and conifer needles are examples of plant parts in the litter layer. Underneath the litter layer is the humus or duff layer. This layer is a dark, light-textured organic material that has decomposed to such an extent that plant parts can no longer be recognized.

The thickness of the litter and duff layers are measured at the north, south, east, and west edges of the sampling frame. The forest floor (subplots 2, 3, and 4) is then sampled by collecting all organic materials less than 0.64 cm (1/4 inch) in diameter within a 30-cm- (12-inch-) diameter sampling frame. Only organic material within this size range is collected; rocks and larger woody materials are discarded.

5.2.2 Upper 20 cm of soils

Once the forest floor has been removed, mineral and organic soils are sampled volumetrically on subplot 2 using an impact-driven bulk density corer (AMS Core Sampler Model #910) with an internal diameter of 4.8 cm. Two 10-cm-long plastic or stainless steel liners are inserted inside of the core head before sampling and used to divide core samples into two sections: 0-10 cm and 10-20 cm. Soils that cannot be sampled with the impact-driven corer (e.g., rocky soils, wetland soils) are sampled using a nonvolumetric excavation method. Soils are collected only if the soil sampling location is forested. The texture of each layer is estimated in the field and characterized as organic, loamy, clayey, sandy, or coarse sandy (see section 4.2.2).

5.2.3 Organic soils

In the FIA program, the term "organic" is used to designate a soil with more than 20 cm of organic material overlying mineral soil, bedrock, or water. These soils are primarily associated with wetlands and are prevalent in certain regions of the country. The term "organic" as used in FIA should not be confused with an organic horizon (or O horizon) as commonly designated in soil terminology. On organic soils, only the litter, and not the entire volume of the forest floor, is collected from the sampling frame. Crews attempt to collect a soil sample using the impact-driven corer. However, in many cases, this will not be possible without severely compacting the sample. If compaction occurs, or if crews have difficulty in obtaining a complete core, samples may be collected at the 0- to 10-cm and 10- to 20-cm depth increments using a Dutch auger or shovel.

5.3 Variables Used to Assess Soil Physical Properties

5.3.1 Forest floor thickness

The thickness of the forest floor and litter layers are used in calculating bulk density values for forest floor samples and in expanding C concentrations to a volumetric basis. When collecting soil samples, field crews record the thickness of the forest floor measured from the top of the litter layer to the boundary between the forest floor and mineral soil. Measurements are made at the north, east, west, and south edges of a 30-cm- (12-in-) diameter circular sampling frame (for a total of four measurements). Where bare soil or bedrock material is exposed, a depth of "0" is recorded. Forest floor thicknesses are collected from soil sampling sites adjacent to subplots 2, 3, and 4. Additional information on forest floor thickness is collected as part of the FIA down woody materials indicator (Woodall and Williams 2005).

5.3.2 Moisture content

Gravimetric soil moisture content is determined for each soil sample. Samples are shipped to the lab immediately after field collection and sealed in plastic bags to prevent the loss of soil moisture. When they arrive in the lab, the field-moist samples are weighed and dried at ambient temperature to a constant weight. Drying time varies depending upon the moisture content and the physical properties of the sample. After being reweighed, a subsample split of the air-dried sample is placed into an oven where it is dried at a temperature of 105°C for 24 hours.

Air (θ_{AD}) and residual (θ_{OD}) moisture contents are then calculated as:

$$\theta_{AD} = \frac{FM}{AD} - 1 \qquad (3)$$

$$\theta_{OD} = \frac{AD_s}{OD_s} - 1 \qquad (4)$$

where FM is the field-moist sample weight (g), AD is the air-dry sample weight (g), AD_s is the air-dry weight of the moisture subsplit (g), and OD_s is the oven-dry weight of the subsplit (g).

θ_{OD} is used to express the weight of the entire sample on an oven-dry basis (SW_{OD}), following:

$$SW_{OD} = \frac{AD}{(\theta_{OD}+1)} \qquad (5)$$

Total moisture content for the entire sample θ_T is then calculated as:

$$\theta_T = (\frac{FM}{SW_{OD}} - 1) * 100 \qquad (6)$$

5.3.3 Bulk density (see also section 3.2.3)

Bulk density is the weight of a unit volume of dry soil, typically expressed in units of grams per cubic centimeter (g cm^{-3}). In addition to providing important information about soil aeration and rooting strength, bulk density is the primary parameter used to scale soil chemical data (expressed in g element g^{-1} soil) to a volumetric (e.g., g cm^{-3}) or areal (e.g., Mg ha^{-1}) basis that is more meaningful for analysis of plant nutrition. Typical bulk density values for a range of soil types and soil materials are provided in table 5.

Bulk density is a calculated variable that requires volumetric sampling in the field and quantitative measurement of soil moisture content. In FIA, bulk density is determined for all mineral and organic soil samples by using an impact-driven corer to collect a sample of known volume from the soil sampling site adjacent to subplot 2. Samples are sent to one of three regional labs for determining moisture content (see discussion of moisture content above). Bulk density (BD_M; g cm^{-3}) is then calculated as:

$$BD_M = \frac{SW_{OD}}{V} \qquad (7)$$

where V is the volume of the soil core (181 cm^3).

For forest floor and litter samples, volumetric samples are collected by measuring the thickness of the forest floor at four points along the outer edge of a 30-cm- (12-in-) diameter sampling frame and then collecting all of the organic material less than 0.64 cm (1/4 inch) in diameter within the sampling frame. The sample is submitted to the lab where it is weighed and a residual moisture content is determined. Bulk density for forest floor samples (BD_F) may be calculated as:

$$BD_F = \frac{SW_{OD}}{(T \times A)} \qquad (8)$$

where T is the mean thickness of the forest floor (cm) and A is the area of the sampling frame (cm).

5.3.4 Coarse fragment content

By convention, soil chemical analyses are conducted only on particles < 2 mm in diameter. To accurately assess the soil chemical concentrations, it is necessary to know what fraction of the sample was composed of particles > 2 mm in diameter. The presence of coarse fragments in the soil also influences aeration and drainage properties, and this variable may be useful in assessing soils that may have lower moisture holding capacities or excessive internal drainage. For a given texture, soils with high coarse fragment content may have a higher bulk density than soils with low coarse fragment content.

Coarse fragment content is measured by sieving air-dried mineral soil samples through a 2 mm mesh and determining the weight of the > 2 mm fraction. This weight is then expressed as a percentage of the total air-dry sample weight.

$$CF = \frac{C_w}{AD} \times 100 \qquad (9)$$

where Cw is the weight of the > 2 mm fraction (g).

5.3.5 Depth to restrictive horizon

The depth to a restrictive horizon is used to indicate the potential for physical barriers in the soil that might impede plant rooting or drainage. In this context, a restrictive horizon is defined as any soil condition that increases soil density to the extent that it might limit root growth. This limitation may be caused by physical properties (hard rock), chemical properties (acid layer), or both.

Measurements of depth to a restrictive horizon are collected on subplots 2, 3, and 4 within the 12-inch diameter area sampled for forest floor chemistry. Crews insert a tile probe into five locations within the soil sampling area (center, north, east, south, and west edges) and push it into the soil to identify whether a restrictive horizon exists. The maximum depth for testing is 50 cm (20 in). If a restrictive layer is encountered within the upper 50 cm of the soil, the median depth (cm) measured at these five points is recorded. If a restrictive

horizon is not encountered, the variable is assigned a value of "50." Crews assign a code of "00" if surficial bedrock is present and "99" if too many rock fragments or cobbles prevent them from inserting the soil probe.

5.4 Variables Used to Assess Chemical Properties

Mineral soil samples collected on FIA plots are analyzed for a suite of physical and chemical properties (table 14). Each of these variables, the methods used in analysis, and guidance for interpretation of results are described in the following section. However, a complete discussion of lab procedures is beyond the scope of this report. Documentation of laboratory procedures (Amacher *et al.* 2003) may be obtained by contacting the authors of this report or your regional FIA program.

Table 14.—*Physical and chemical analyses conducted on mineral soils*[1]

Chemical soil property	Method	Units	Reference
Soil pH	Measurement with a combination pH electrode in a 1:1 soil-water suspension (1:2 soil-water suspension for high organic matter samples)	pH units	Thomas (1996)
Salt pH	Measurement with a combination pH electrode in a 1:1 soil-0.01 M $CaCl_2$ suspension	pH units	Thomas (1996)
Exchangeable cations (Na, K, Mg, Ca, Al) and S	1 M NH_4Cl extraction with ICP-OES analysis	mg kg^{-1}	Sumner and Miller (1996); Amacher *et al.* (1990)
Trace metals (Mn, Fe, Ni, Cu, Zn, Cd, and Pb)	1 M NH_4Cl extraction with ICP-OES analysis	mg kg^{-1}	Sumner and Miller (1996); Amacher *et al.* (1990)
Extractable P for soils with pH < 6	Bray-1 (0.03 M NH_4F + 0.025 M HCl) extraction with colorimetric analysis by ascorbic acid method	mg kg^{-1}	Kuo (1996); Soil and Plant Analysis Council (1999)
Extractable P for soils with pH > 6	Olsen (pH 8.5, 0.5 M $NaHCO_3$) extraction with colorimetric analysis by ascorbic acid method	mg kg^{-1}	Kuo (1996); Soil and Plant Analysis Council (1999)
Total C	Combustion analyzer for total C (preferred for forest floor and noncalcareous mineral soil samples)	%	Soil Survey Laboratory (1996)
Organic and inorganic C	Combustion analyzer for multiple forms of C (preferred for calcareous mineral soil samples)	%	Amacher *et al.* (2003)
Organic C only	Dichromate oxidation with heating	%	Nelson and Sommers (1996)
Inorganic C (carbonates) only	Pressure calcimeter	%	Sherrod *et al.* (2002)
Total N	Combustion analyzer	%	Soil Survey Laboratory (1996)

[1] Additional detail is available in Amacher *et al.* (2003).

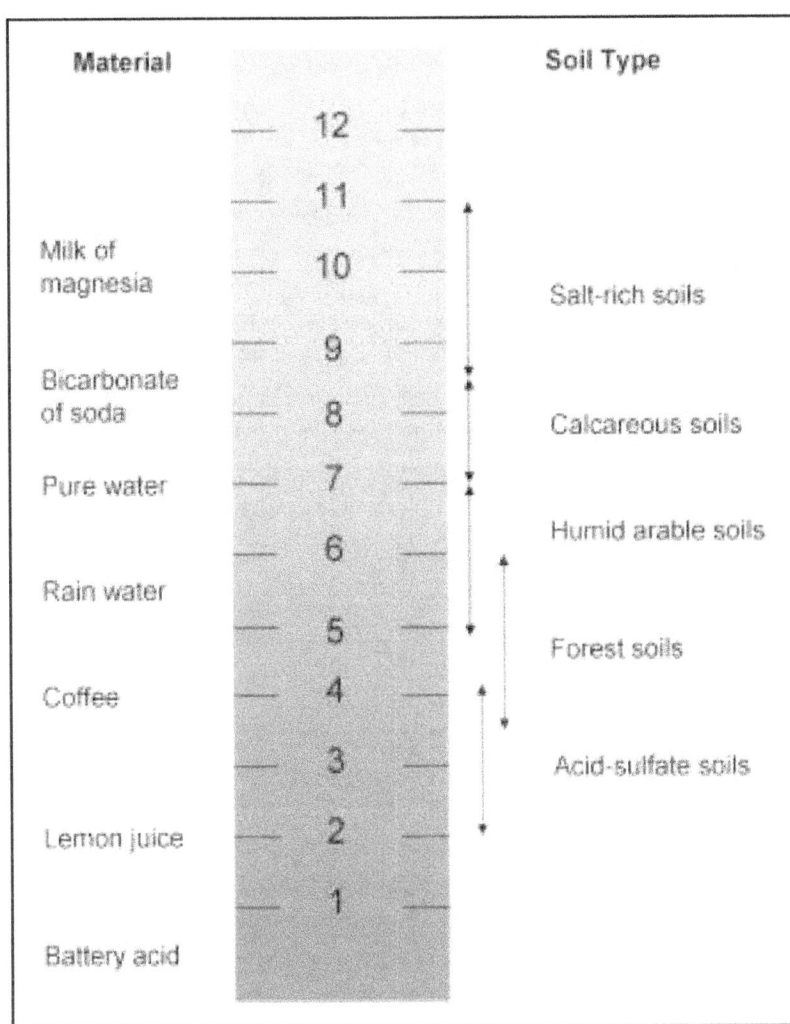

Figure 11.—pH ranges for common materials and soil types. [Figure adapted from Brady and Weil (1996).]

5.4.1 Soil acidity (pH)

Soil pH is often referred to as a "master variable" because it influences nearly all physical, chemical, and biological processes in the soil. Soil pH is a measure of hydrogen ion activity (H^+) equal to:

$$pH = -\log (H^+) \qquad (10)$$

where (H^+) refers to the activity of the hydrogen ion. The pH scale ranges from 0 to 14, with pH 7.0 as the neutral point. The more acidic a soil is, the lower its pH value. The scale for pH is logarithmic such that each 1-unit change in pH correlates to a tenfold change in soil acidity. Examples of pH ranges for common substances are found in figure 11.

Soil pH is a primary factor in determining the fertility of the soil through its regulation of soil nutrient availability, aggregate stability, and microbial activity. Both natural and human activities can influence soil pH. For example, chemical fertilizers and organic wastes added to the soil can react with water in the soil solution to form strong acids that increase soil acidity. Similarly, acid deposition associated with the combustion of fossil fuels forms when gases containing N and S are introduced into the atmosphere where they combine with water to form nitric and sulfuric acid. In soils that are poorly buffered against acidic inputs, toxic quantities of Al may be mobilized and important plant nutrients such as Ca may become depleted. Over time, forest species may become weakened or even killed.

Soil acidity may be divided into three general categories (Brady and Weil 1996):

Active acidity (water pH) A measure of the H^+ activity in the soil at a given time.

Salt-replaceable acidity (salt pH) Associated with the exchangeable Al^{3+} and H^+ on soil colloids. These ions can be released into the soil solution by unbuffered salt solutions.

Residual acidity The acidity that remains in the soil after the active and salt-replaceable acidity has been neutralized. Generally associated with H^+ and Al^{3+} ions bound in nonexchangeable forms.

FIA analyzes soils for both active and salt-replaceable pH. Air-dried and prepared mineral soil samples are mixed with deionized water in a 1:1 ratio (1 mL water per 1 g air dried soil) to form a slurry and allowed to sit for 30 minutes; organic soil samples are mixed at a 2:1 ratio. The water pH of the slurry is then measured using a pH meter and electrode. Samples are then spiked with 200 μL of 1 M $CaCl_2$, allowed to sit for another 30 minutes, and remeasured to determine salt pH. Measurements are made to the nearest 0.1 pH unit.

Acidification of the soil in response to pollution and acid deposition is an issue of great concern in some regions of the country. Although the FIA soils data provide critical monitoring data to assess the impacts of acidification, the effects of acid deposition cannot be determined by looking solely at the current pH of the soil. Soil pH varies as a function of factors such as clay mineralogy, soil age, weathering status, climate, vegetation, and organic matter. For example, highly weathered soils in the Southeast may have very low pH values that do not indicate a forest health problem. However, if these same low pH values were found in naturally alkaline soils of the Upper Midwest, it might well indicate cause for concern. The ability of a particular soil to withstand changes in pH is primarily a function of the acid neutralizing capacity of the soil and the dominant clay mineralogy. For this reason, acidification needs to be evaluated within the context of soil type and must incorporate other soil chemical parameters such as exchangeable Al and S.

Many of the available soil maps and surveys are based largely upon analysis of agricultural soils, and care must be taken when comparing pH values from forested soils to survey data. In general, forest soils tend to be naturally more acidic than agricultural soils due to the higher levels of organic acids produced by decomposition and leaching through the forest floor.

5.4.2 Exchangeable cations

Clay minerals and organic matter in the soil function as potential reservoirs for plant nutrients because they have a net negative charge. Negatively charged exchange sites on the surface of soil particles bind with positively charged ions (cations) in the soil solution (e.g., Na^+, Mg^{2+}, Ca^{2+}). These cations are not permanently bound to the particle and can be replaced by other cations as the chemistry of the soil solution changes. The cation exchange capacity (CEC) refers to the total number of exchangeable cations that a soil can hold, and is equivalent to the amount of its negative charge. The higher the CEC, the more cations a soil can retain.

The nutrient holding capacity of a particular soil depends upon a number of factors, including texture, mineralogy, and pH. Only clays and organic matter carry a negative charge and are capable of contributing to the CEC. As a result, fine-textured soils will generally have higher CECs than sandier soils. Different clay minerals also have different CECs. In general, the more highly weathered the clay mineral, the lower the CEC. Because of this strong association with texture and mineralogy, the spatial distribution of nutrient holding capacity closely follows the underlying geology of the parent material. Finally, the CEC of a soil varies as a function of pH. Soil exchange sites preferentially adsorb H^+ ions, and as the number of H^+ ions in solution increases (pH decreases), the number of exchange sites available for nutrient retention declines. As a result, these nutrients may leach through the soil where they become unavailable for plant uptake.

FIA determines exchangeable base cation concentrations based on an extraction with an unbuffered solution of ammonium chloride (NH_4Cl). The extract solution is then analyzed by ICP-OES (inductively coupled plasma optical emission spectroscopy). Results are expressed in units of milligram of cation per kilogram of soil.

Reporting of cation data from Phase 3 plots depends highly on the method used, and any reporting should specify both the method and extractant used. One of the more commonly used methods for determining exchangeable cations uses an ammonium acetate (NH_4OAc)

extraction buffered at a pH of 7.0 or 8.2, depending on which version of the method is used. By buffering the extract at such a high pH, there is little effect of pH-dependent charge. However, few forest soils have a pH of 8.2 or even 7.0 in the field, and this cation concentration represents a maximum value. In the FIA method, the pH of the solution varies depending upon the pH of the sample, and extraction provides a more accurate representation of the CEC under field conditions. An additional advantage of the NH_4Cl method is that Al, S, and trace metals may also be determined from the same extraction, greatly reducing analysis time and lab expenses. However, it also means that the exchangeable cations measured at a given site may have a higher degree of variability from year to year than when measured by a buffered extraction. As a result of differences in methods, cation concentrations reported in the literature may be higher than those reported by FIA.

5.4.2.1 Exchangeable potassium

Potassium (K^+) is one of the three major plant nutrients (along with N and P). In addition to functioning as a primary component in the gas exchange mechanism of plants by facilitating the operations of the stomata, K^+ plays a role in the synthesis of starch and the translocation of carbohydrates in plants. Potassium is also essential to a plant's capacity to resist disease, survive cold temperatures, and provide drought protection (Potash and Phosphate Institute 1995). Although most soils contain large amounts of K^+ in clay minerals and rocks, the majority of this is unavailable for plant uptake (Brady and Weil 1996). FIA measures only the exchangeable, or plant-available, forms of K^+ that are found in the soil solution or held in an exchangeable form by soil organic matter and clay.

5.4.2.2 Exchangeable calcium

Calcium (Ca^{2+}) is used by plants for a variety of functions, including stimulation of root and leaf development, formation of cell walls, enzyme activation, and neutralization of organic acids. Deficiencies can result in poor root growth and gelatinous leaf tips and growing points (Taiz and Zeiger 1991). However, deficiencies are rarely observed in the field because secondary effects such as low pH usually limit growth first (Potash and Phosphate Institute 1995). Calcium is the

dominant cation in most neutral to alkaline forest floor solutions and typically occupies 70-90 percent of soil exchange sites (Fisher and Binkley 2000). Total amounts of Ca^{2+} in the soil range from less than 0.1 percent in newly drained organic soils to as much as 25 percent in calcareous soils of arid regions (Potash and Phosphate Institute 1995).

5.4.2.3 Exchangeable magnesium

Magnesium (Mg^{2+}) is a key element required for plant photosynthesis because of its role as the central atom in the chlorophyll molecule (Potash and Phosphate Institute 1995, Taiz and Zeiger 1991). Magnesium is also involved in phosphate metabolism, plant respiration, and the activation of many enzyme systems. Deficiencies are often associated with coarse-textured, acidic soils in regions of high precipitation. In soils with a low CEC, Mg^{2+} uptake may be reduced by high Ca^{2+} concentrations, resulting in plant deficiencies (Potash and Phosphate Institute 1995).

5.4.2.4 Exchangeable sodium

High concentrations of Na^+ in the soil may be detrimental both physically and chemically. At high levels, Na^+ tends to break apart soil aggregates. These dispersed clay particles clog the soil pores as they move through the profile, reducing water and air infiltration. In addition, plant growth on salt-affected soils tends to be limited by high levels of Na^+, OH^-, and HCO_3^- ions (Brady and Weil 1996). Because Na^+ may easily be leached from the upper part of the soil profile in areas with high rates of precipitation, exchangeable Na^+ tends to be greatest in arid regions such as the Western U.S.

5.4.2.5 Exchangeable aluminum

At very low pH values (pH < 5.0), Al in clay minerals becomes soluble and exists as positively charged aluminum (Al^{3+}) or aluminum hydroxy (e.g., $Al(OH)^{2+}$, $Al(OH)_2^+$) cations. These cations can become adsorbed on negatively charged clay particles in the same way that base cations do (Brady and Weil 1996). Aluminum ions can react with water molecules to release H+ ions into solution and increase soil acidity (lower pH). For example:

$$Al^{3+} + H_2O \Leftrightarrow AlOH^{2+} + H^+ \qquad (11)$$

Each Al^{3+} ion can produce three H^+ ions, greatly decreasing soil pH (Sparks 1995). In addition to its effects on soil acidity, Al is toxic to some plants and can cause roots to become short and stunted (Taiz and Zeiger 1991). Susceptibility to Al toxicity varies by species.

5.4.2.6 Effective cation exchange capacity

Effective cation exchange capacity (ECEC) reflects the CEC of soils after the effects of salt-extractable acidity have been removed. In practice, ECEC is determined as the sum of exchangeable base cations plus exchangeable Al:

$$ECEC = \sum [Ca^{2+}], [Na^+], [Mg^{2+}], [K^+], [Al^{3+}] \quad (12)$$

ECEC is expressed in terms of milligram equivalents per 100 g of soil (meq/100 g) or centimoles of charge per kilogram of soil ($cmol_c\ kg^{-1}$); the two units are equivalent. ECEC is a useful index of total nutrient holding capacity in a particular soil and will vary as a function of clay mineralogy, weathering status, and soil pH.

5.4.3 Extractable phosphorus

Phosphorus (P) is an essential component of nearly all metabolic processes in both plants and animals. Phosphorus forms a high-energy bond in the organic compound ATP (adenosine triphosphate), which drives most energy-dependent biochemical reactions (Brady and Weil 1996). In addition, P is a key component of DNA and cellular membranes (Taiz and Zeiger 1991). Despite its great importance in plant metabolism, soil P is frequently bound in forms unavailable for plant uptake and may become a limiting factor for site productivity (Brady and Weil 1996).

Determination of P availability depends highly on the method used. Extractants used in soil P determination estimate the capacity of the soil to provide P by dissolving and/or desorbing a particular fraction of the labile P. Unlike other soil nutrients measured in FIA that are found as positively charged ions (e.g., Ca^{2+}, Mg^+, Na^+), P typically occurs as part of the negatively charged phosphate complex (PO_4^-). Since clay particles and organic matter are also negatively charged, the bonding mechanisms for P are more complex (Brady and Weil 1996, Sparks 1995).

FIA measures extractable P on all mineral soil samples. Soils are extracted with a solution tailored to the type of dominant P mineralogy in the soils, filtered, and then analyzed colorimetrically. The extractant used in this analysis varies depending upon the pH. A Bray-1 extractant (0.03 M NH_4F + 0.025 M HCl) is used for soils with a pH < 6.0. Near-neutral and alkaline soils (pH > 6.0) are extracted following the Olsen method (pH 8.5, 0.5 M $NaHCO_3$). Results are reported in units of milligrams of P per kilogram of soil.

5.4.4 Total nitrogen

Nitrogen (N), a key factor in the development of leaf area, regulates the amount of photosynthate available for plant growth and reproduction, and increases the protein content of plants. Yet, despite its great importance in plant nutrition, the amount of available N in the soil is small. The majority of soil N is contained in soil organic matter (organic N) in a form that is unavailable to plants. Plant-available soil N (inorganic N) is produced when microorganisms mineralize organic forms of N. The two primary resulting ions are ammonium (NH_4^+) and nitrate (NO_3^-); some plant species prefer NH_4^+ nutrition while others utilize NO_3^- (Marschner 1986). This plant-available N represents 2-3 percent of the total amount of N in the soil (Potash and Phosphate Institute 1995).

In FIA, total soil N is measured by dry combustion. A small sample of air-dried soil is combusted in a pure oxygen (O) atmosphere. The combustion products are separated and quantified by passing them through a packed column. Results are expressed as a percentage of air-dry sample weight. When interpreting total-N data, it is important to keep in mind that the majority of this N is not available for plant uptake. Total-N data should be used only as an index of soil N availability.

5.4.5 Total, organic, and inorganic carbon

Soil organic matter is important for water retention, C sequestration, and soil organisms and is an indication of soil nutrient status (Brady and Weil 1996). Changes in soil organic matter or nutrients can affect the vitality of forest ecosystems through diminished regeneration capacity of trees, lower growth rates, and changes in species composition. The accumulation of biomass as living vegetation, debris, peat, and soil C is an important forest function in regulating atmospheric C concentrations. The production rate of biomass is also a measure of forest health and vitality.

FIA analyzes soils for total C concentration by dry combustion following the method outlined above for total N. Results are expressed as a percent of air-dry sample weight. In high pH soils, some fraction of total C may be derived from inorganic carbonates in the soil parent material. Mineral soils with a pH > 7.5 are analyzed for either inorganic (TIC) or organic carbon (TOC), depending on the instrumentation at the lab, and the remaining pool is determined by subtraction from total carbon (TC):

$$TC = TIC + TOC \qquad (13)$$

One of the objectives of the soil indicator is to provide a mechanism for monitoring changes in soil organic matter and C sequestration in response to management practices and disturbances. Inorganic C does not represent C sequestered in the system as a result of plant activity, and only organic C concentrations should be used for developing C budgets. Details on converting concentrations to volumetric and areal estimates are provided in section 5.5.

5.4.6 C:N ratio

The ratio of organic C to N is frequently used by ecologists as an index of litter quality (Brady and Weil 1996, Fisher and Binkley 2000, Waring and Schlesinger 1985). The majority of soil microorganisms obtain their energy by metabolizing soil C (decomposition). During this process, they withdraw nutrients from the soil. On average, soil microorganisms must incorporate 1 part of N for every 8 parts of C metabolized (C:N ratio of 8:1). As a result, the C:N ratio of organic matter tends to decline as organic material becomes more highly decomposed (Brady and Weil 1996, Schlesinger 1991). For reference, C:N ratios from common organic materials are provided in table 15.

Table 15.—*C:N ratios from common organic materials[1]*

Organic material	C:N ratio
Spruce sawdust	600:1
Hardwood sawdust	400:1
Wheat straw	80:1
Household compost	16:1
Average B horizon (mineral soil)	9:1
Soil bacteria	5:1

[1] Adapted from Brady and Weil (1996).

5.4.7 Extractable sulfur

Sulfur (S) is a constituent of many amino acids and is closely associated with N in protein and enzyme formation. Both inadequate and excess amounts of S in the soil can cause forest health problems (Potash and Phosphate Institute 1995, Taiz and Zeiger 1991). Plant-available S (inorganic S) in soil occurs as the SO_4^{2-} anion. Because of this negative charge, SO_4^{2-} is not usually adsorbed onto soil particles and remains in the soil solution where it can be removed by leaching (Brady and Weil 1996). In the United States, deficiencies of S are most commonly observed in the Southeast, the Pacific Northwest, and the Great Plains. Soils in regions with a high concentration of heavy industry, such as the Northeast, are less likely to be deficient in S (Brady and Weil 1996).

At an ecosystem level, excess S is associated with several types of air and water pollution that can result in forest decline and other health problems. High levels of atmospheric S are associated with industry and the combustion of fossil fuels. Some of these materials can become oxidized in the atmosphere to form sulfuric acid and sulfate salts, which are then deposited in forests through wet and dry deposition (Waring and Schlesinger 1985). Elevated levels of atmospheric S, and the acidification that these compounds can cause in the soil, may result in serious damage to forest ecosystems (Schlesinger 1991). In combination with information about pH and exchangeable Al, analysis of temporal trends in soil S concentration relative to background levels will provide needed information for monitoring the effects of acid deposition on forest soils.

5.4.8 Micronutrients and trace metals (Mn, Fe, Ni, Cu, Zn, Cd, Pb)

Although required in smaller quantities, micronutrients may be just as important to plant nutrition as major nutrients. Micronutrients measured in FIA include manganese (Mn), iron (Fe), copper (Cu), and zinc (Zn). Some of the additional metals selected for analysis can be used to address Criterion 4, Indicator 25: Area and percent of forest land experiencing an accumulation of persistent toxic substances. These include nickel (Ni), cadmium (Cd), and lead (Pb).

Micronutrients and trace metals are determined by extraction of air-dried mineral soils with a 1 M NH$_4$Cl solution and analysis on ICP. Analysis is concurrent with exchangeable cations (see section 5.4.2). At present, the suite of metals analyzed varies depending on lab instrumentation.

5.5 Analysis and Interpretation

FIA chemical data are available in online databases and will be included in FIA State and regional reports. Table 16 and table 17 provide an example of how soils data may be reported at the State level. Although data can be reported in tables, information about changes in soil chemical and physical properties is likely to be more meaningful to managers and researchers when reported within maps. Soil chemical and physical data needs to be analyzed in conjunction with other physical and chemical characteristics, soil type, and ecosystem. Mapped products allow for the integration of monitoring data with soil survey data and/or other base mapping products such as ecoregion section or subsection and provide the

landscape perspective that is critical to interpreting soils data. There is no reason to expect that soil type is directly related to forest cover type, and aggregation of soils data into cover classes for reporting purposes may mask important trends. Regardless of how the data are presented, interpretation of a single chemical variable in isolation may result in misleading findings.

5.5.1 Unit conversions

Elemental data from soil analyses are typically expressed in units of concentration (e.g., %, mg kg^{-1}, cmol$_c$ kg^{-1}). However, because plants exist within a volume of soil, units of volume may be more ecologically meaningful for addressing forest health questions. Concentration data are converted to volumetric units by using the soil bulk density (weight soil per unit volume). Mathematically, this conversion can be represented as:

$$E_{VOL} = [E] \times BD \qquad (14)$$

where E$_{VOL}$ is the element of interest expressed volumetrically (g cm^{-3}), [E] is the elemental

Table 16.—*Example table for reporting physical properties of forest floor and mineral soils by forest type group*

Soil layer and forest type group	Number of samples	Depth to subsoil	% coarse fragments	Forest floor thickness (cm)	Bulk density (g/cm^3)
Forest floor					
Elm/ash/cottonwood group	3	—	—	2.02	—
Loblolly/shortleaf pine group	2	—	—	5.80	—
Maple/beech/birch group	2	—	—	4.52	—
Oak/hickory group	83	—	—	4.76	—
Oak/pine group	5	—	—	3.58	—
Pinyon/juniper group	3	—	—	5.78	—
All forest type groups	98	—	—	4.66	—
Mineral (0-10 cm)					
Elm/ash/cottonwood group	2	38.96	1.26	—	1.26
Loblolly/shortleaf pine group	1	19.40	48.69	—	1.39
Oak/hickory group	63	17.33	23.94	—	1.20
Oak/pine group	4	13.53	31.57	—	1.13
All forest type groups	70	18.24	23.73	—	1.20
Mineral (10-20 cm)					
Elm/ash/cottonwood group	2	—	1.04	—	1.55
Loblolly/shortleaf pine group	1	—	47.56	—	1.43
Oak/hickory group	61	—	27.28	—	1.56
Oak/pine group	4	—	49.89	—	1.57
All forest type groups	68	—	27.61	—	1.56

All table cells without observations in the inventory sample are indicated by —. Table value of 0.0 indicates the volume rounds to less than 0.01.
Columns and rows may not add to their totals due to rounding.

Table 17.—Example table for reporting chemical properties of forest floor and mineral soils by forest type group

Soil layer and forest type group	Number of samples	pH H₂O	pH CaCl₂	Organic carbon (%)	Inorganic carbon (%)	Total nitrogen (%)	Extractable phosphorus (mg/kg)	Extractable cations (cmolc/kg) Na	K	Mg	Ca	Al	ECEC	Extractable sulfur (mg/kg)
Forest floor														
Elm/ash/cottonwood group	3	—	—	28.50	—	1.09	—	—	—	—	—	—	—	—
Loblolly/shortleaf pine group	2	—	—	31.78	—	0.88	—	—	—	—	—	—	—	—
Maple/beech/birch group	2	—	—	30.03	—	1.26	—	—	—	—	—	—	—	—
Oak/hickory group	81	—	—	33.20	—	1.15	—	—	—	—	—	—	—	—
Oak/pine group	5	—	—	34.10	—	1.16	—	—	—	—	—	—	—	—
Pinyon/juniper group	3	—	—	33.42	—	1.26	—	—	—	—	—	—	—	—
All forest type groups	94	—	—	33.04	—	1.15	—	—	—	—	—	—	—	—
Mineral (0-10 cm)														
Elm/ash/cottonwood group	2	6.76	6.42	2.00	0.01	0.14	2.26	15.00	190.50	302.50	2,264.50	—	14.34	6.65
Loblolly/shortleaf pine group	2	5.38	4.92	3.32	—	0.21	3.31	8.60	81.00	246.20	1,254.60	4.60	8.59	10.52
Oak/hickory group	66	5.44	4.88	3.06	—	0.19	5.24	14.10	103.60	169.99	1,088.23	69.69	7.93	8.92
Oak/pine group	4	5.75	5.30	3.98	—	0.26	4.11	17.46	111.77	371.62	1,846.23	5.77	12.70	9.00
Pinyon/juniper group	1	6.97	6.57	4.66	—	0.32	—	11.00	240.00	970.00	3,615.00	—	26.68	9.00
All forest type groups	75	5.51	4.97	3.10	—	0.19	4.99	14.14	108.11	196.57	1,198.75	62.40	8.63	8.89
Mineral (10-20 cm)														
Elm/ash/cottonwood group	2	6.24	5.69	1.09	0.02	0.10	0.72	11.00	98.50	206.50	1,397.50	30.00	9.31	4.05
Loblolly/shortleaf pine group	2	5.20	4.67	1.54	—	0.12	2.00	8.20	49.80	147.40	575.60	33.00	4.62	6.76
Oak/hickory group	63	5.24	4.57	1.20	—	0.09	4.96	14.68	70.71	135.81	676.47	105.10	5.90	7.15
Oak/pine group	4	5.79	5.19	2.24	—	0.17	3.04	23.62	79.38	377.77	1,199.46	5.38	9.46	6.69
Pinyon/juniper group	1	7.11	6.69	2.96	—	0.23	—	11.00	215.00	1,030.00	3,535.00	—	26.71	7.00
All forest type groups	72	5.33	4.67	1.28	—	0.10	4.60	14.83	73.79	163.82	766.06	94.89	6.48	7.02

All table cells without observations in the inventory sample are indicated by —. Table value of 0 indicates the value rounds to less than 0.01. Columns and rows may not add to their totals due to rounding.
ECEC = Effective cation exchange capacity.
Extractable phosphorus is reported for the Bray-1 method. Results for the Olsen method are also available.

concentration determined from laboratory analysis, and BD is the sample bulk density (g cm^{-3}). Additional conversion factors may also be necessary depending on the reporting units for a particular element. Conversion factors for soil chemical data are summarized in table 18.

In some applications, elemental data are expressed on an areal basis. For example, C and N budgets are typically expressed in units of weight area^{-1} (e.g., kg m^{-2}, Mg ha^{-1}). Conversion of volumetric data to an areal basis requires multiplication by the thickness of soil represented by the sample core. For example:

$$E_s = \%E \times BD \times T \qquad (15)$$

where E_s = elemental storage, %E is the weight percent of the element, BD is the bulk density (g cm^{-3}), and T is the thickness of the sample (cm). In FIA, mineral soil samples are collected using a 10-cm core, such that T = 10. Depending on the analysis, it may be desirable to adjust elemental data for the coarse fragment content. This may be done by modifying Equation 15, following:

$$E_s = \%E \times BD \times T \times (1-S) \qquad (16)$$

where S is the volume of the coarse fragment fraction (> 2 mm diameter). For forest floors,

samples are collected from a known area rather than a known volume, so concentrations are converted to an areal basis by multiplying by the ratio of the sample weight to the area of the sampling frame, following:

$$E_s = \%E \times \frac{SW_{OD}}{A} \qquad (17)$$

where E_s is elemental storage, %E is the weight percent of the element, SW_{OD} is the oven-dry sample weight, and A is the area of the sampling frame.

5.6 Examples of Analyses

To illustrate how soil chemical data may be used in FIA, FHM, or other reporting efforts, 383 plots sampled in the Southeastern U.S. in 1998 and 1999 were evaluated for organic matter storage and pH. For upper mineral soils (defined as "A Horizons" in 1998 and 0-10 cm in 1999), 60.3 percent of the plots (231 out of 383) had organic C values of less than or equal to 3 percent (fig. 12). Highest C concentrations were associated with the mountainous regions of Virginia and West Virginia and central Alabama (fig. 12). Carbon data may also be aggregated by soil order and masked using a forest-nonforest GIS to produce an integrated estimate of C storage within the forest floor and upper 20 cm of mineral soils at the regional scale (O'Neill *et al.* 2004; O'Neill *et al.*, in progress[1]).

Table 18.—*Factors for converting soil chemical concentrations in areal units*

Element	Units reported	Conversion factor[1] (kg m^{-2})
pH	pH units	None
Carbon (total, inorganic, organic)	Weight % (g C per g soil)	Bulk density (g cm^{-3}) * 100
Total nitrogen (N)	Weight % (g N per g soil)	Bulk density (g cm^{-3}) * 100
Extractable phosphorus (P)	mg P per kg soil	Bulk density (g cm^{-3}) * 0.0001
Calcium (Ca^{2+})	mg Ca^{2+} per kg soil	Bulk density (g cm^{-3}) * 0.0001
Magnesium (Mg^{2+})	mg Mg^{2+} per kg soil	Bulk density (g cm^{-3}) * 0.0001
Potassium (K$^+$)	mg K$^+$ per kg soil	Bulk density (g cm^{-3}) * 0.0001
Sodium (Na$^+$)	mg Na^{2+} per kg soil	Bulk density (g cm^{-3}) * 0.0001
Sulfur (S)	mg S per kg soil	Bulk density (g cm^{-3}) * 0.0001
Aluminum (Al)	mg Al per kg soil	Bulk density (g cm^{-3}) * 0.0001
Other base cations	mg cation per kg soil	Bulk density (g cm^{-3}) * 0.0001

[1] Assumes a 10-cm core thickness.

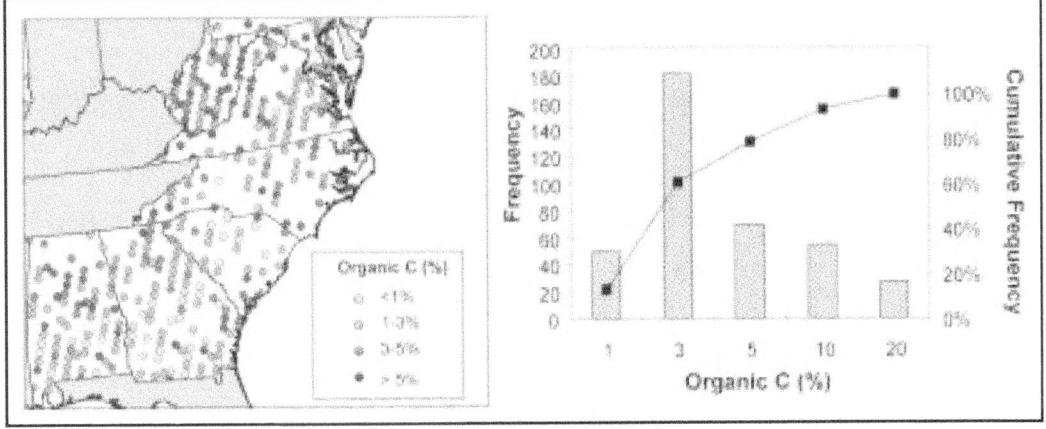

Figure 12.—Organic carbon values for 0- to 10-cm soils sampled in the Southeastern U.S. from 1998 to 1999.

Samples collected throughout the region indicate that soils were strongly acidic, with only 3 plots (0.8%) having a pH value above 6.0. Nearly one-fifth (17.8% or 68 plots) had a pH value of less than 4.0 (fig. 13). Under these acidic conditions, Al in the soil becomes soluble and may cause toxicity to plants. Soils with the lowest pH values tended to be clustered within the mountains of West Virginia and the coastal plain of North Carolina, South Carolina, and Georgia (fig. 13).

After describing the general trends in soil chemistry, analysts may then compare soil properties with other forest health components, such as growth/mortality ratios, dieback, or indices of air quality from the lichen and ozone indicators to determine whether there is any relationship between soil nutrient content and forest productivity. As remeasurement data become available, analysts may examine regional trends in C, pH, and soil nutrients in conjunction with changes in forest growth and productivity.

5.7 Limitations to Data

Soil chemical and physical properties can be highly variable in the field and are expensive to analyze. As a result, interpretation of soil chemical data is confounded by spatial variability within the plot. In addition, depending upon the soil type, both the number of samples and the methods used in collecting these samples may vary between plots, complicating compilation and estimation procedures. Finally, soil samples reflect conditions only in the forest floor and upper 20 cm of the soil. In many systems, the upper portion of the soil profile is likely to be more responsive to disturbance, providing a useful index for monitoring changes in soil properties over time. However, conclusive answers to forest health questions may require additional analyses of samples taken from within the entire rooting zone.

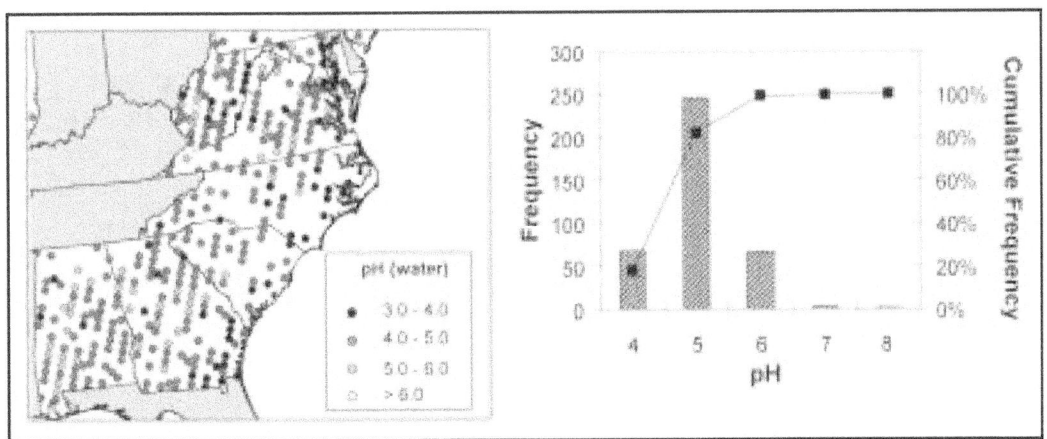

Figure 13.—pH values for 0- to 10-cm soils sampled in the Southeastern U.S. from 1998 to 1999.

6. POTENTIAL PROBLEMS WITH COMBINING DATA FROM MULTIPLE YEARS (1998-2002)

As with any new research program, modifications to the sampling and measurement protocols are a necessary part of indicator development and implementation. During the first 4 years of the soil indicator (1998-2001), evaluation of quality assurance data along with feedback from the field crews, regional trainers, and lab personnel resulted in a series of improvements to the measurement protocol that have enhanced both the efficiency of the program and the data quality. However, these changes also seriously complicate the analysis of data collected across multiple field seasons. Analysts and researchers interested in incorporating data collected before the 2001 field season need to be aware of the ways in which the protocols have changed and account for these interannual differences in their analyses.

Table 8, table 19, and table 20 outline those changes in the field methods, soil sampling protocols, and laboratory analyses that could create difficulties when analyzing and interpreting results. Detailed information about field methods for a given year may be found in the FIA field manuals (contact your regional FIA office for additional information; http://www.fia.fs.fed.us).

Some of the most difficult changes to address analytically occur in the soil chemistry portion of the indicator. Since 1998, the number of samples collected, the depths of these samples, the method used to collect the samples (core vs. shovel), and the laboratory methods used to analyze the samples have all been modified. The net result of these changes is that soil chemical values from samples collected in 1998 and 1999 are not directly comparable with those obtained from samples collected since 2000. In general, combined data from these first 5 years of implementation should not be used to develop baseline statistics for State or regional reporting.

Table 19.—*Changes in soil sampling protocols, 1998-2001*

Year(s) of implementation	Method
Number of samples	
1998–1999	Maximum of 7 samples per plot: 1 forest floor sample (subplot 2); 2 mineral samples each on subplots 2, 3, and 4.
2000	Maximum of 3 samples per plot: 1 forest floor sample and 2 mineral samples from subplot 2 only.
2001–present	Maximum of 5 samples per plot: 3 forest floor samples and 2 mineral samples from subplot 2 only.
Bulk density	
1998–1999	Samples collected using a shovel; no bulk density measurement.
2000	Samples collected using a bulk density sampler in some States.
2001–present	Samples collected using a bulk density sampler in all States.
Mineral soils	
1998	Samples collected by genetic soil horizon.
1999–present	Samples collected by two depth increments (0-10 cm and 10-20 cm).
Forest floor	
1998–1999	If forest floor > 5 cm, then litter and duff sampled separately.
2000–present	Forest floor sampled as single unit.
Composite samples	
1998–2000	Samples from multiple subplots could be composited if in same condition class and soil texture.
2001–present	No compositing.

Table 20.—*Changes in lab protocols, 1998-2001*

Year(s) of implementation	Method
Percent moisture	
1998–1999	Samples frozen prior to stabilization for pest control.
2000–present	Samples air-dried immediately upon arrival at lab.
Extractable phosphorus (P)	
1998–1999	Bray-1 method for all soils.
2000–present	Bray-1 method for soils with pH < 6.0; Olsen method for soils with pH > 6.0.
Base cations	
1998–1999	Ammonium acetate extraction with analysis by atomic absorption spectroscopy (AAS).
2000–present	Ammonium chloride extraction with analysis by inductively coupled plasma optical emissions spectroscopy (ICP-OES).
Aluminum, sulfur, and trace metals	
1998–1999	Not done.
2000–present	Ammonium chloride extraction with analysis by inductively coupled plasma optical emissions spectroscopy (ICP-OES).
pH	
1998–1999	Solid state electrode.
2000–present	Glass bulb electrode.

7. QUALITY ASSURANCE

7.1 Field

Field personnel receive thorough training in field procedures and soil sampling techniques at the beginning of each field season and must pass a method-specific certification test in which they demonstrate the ability to conduct soil measurements within established measurement quality objectives and tolerances. Regional trainers for the soil indictor are certified each year at a national pre-training session conducted by the soil indicator advisors. The purpose of the pre-training session is to ensure national consistency in the dissemination of information and training materials and to minimize regional variations in measurements.

Quality control checks on field data collection are conducted through audits and plot remeasurements throughout the field season. Feedback from the crews and regional coordinators is a key part of the quality assurance program and is critical to identifying and correcting problems with training, data quality, consistency, and methodology. Quality assurance procedures for the field portion of the soil indicator consist of three activities:

Hot Checks (audits)

Auditors observe field crew members during data collection on a field plot, review the methods, identify problems, and suggest any needed corrective actions. Auditors may also conduct independent soil measurements.

Cold Checks

Auditors conduct spot checks on field measurements and compare these to data collected by the crews. Field crews are not present for the audit. Auditors may correct any error that they find in the data.

Blind Checks

The complete remeasurement of a plot by the auditors. Auditors do not have access to the data from the field crew and may not correct any errors. These are used to provide an unbiased estimate of data variance.

Remeasurements of field observations by regional trainer crews occur on routine plots recently visited by a standard field crew (cold checks or hot checks) or on reference plots. A national standard of 5 percent remeasurement has been established for all FIA plots. During a remeasurement, all erosion and soil compaction remeasurements are taken on the subplots as described in the soil measurement methods. However, because of the cost of analysis, soil samples are collected only during blind checks. A national standard for blind checks has been set at a minimum of 10 plots per region.

7.2 Laboratory

Quality control protocols used by the FIA regional labs are documented in Amacher et al. (2003) and include the use of blanks, calibration standards, and independent check standards. Interlaboratory compatibility is ensured through participation in the North American Proficiency Testing program (NAPT) administered by the American Society of Agronomy. The NAPT is a sample exchange program designed to monitor interlaboratory differences and assess overall lab performance. Samples used in the program are contributed from throughout the continental U.S. and represent a wide range of soil types. Because of the large number of labs participating in the program (> 100) and the wide range of soil types analyzed, this program is a robust measure of lab performance.

8. REGULATIONS PERTAINING TO THE SOIL INDICATOR

8.1 Plot Confidentiality

To protect landowner privacy and prevent sampling bias, the locations of FIA plots are kept confidential. These data are exempted from the Freedom of Information Act. Researchers interested in spatial analyses of soil indicator data may contact their regional FIA program office for more information.

8.2 Sample Collection

The National Historic Preservation Act of 1966 (as amended) provides for the protection of historical and cultural artifacts. Because of the random placement of the Phase 3 monitoring design, Phase 3 plots may possibly be located on sites of prehistoric or historical significance. Crews do not collect soil samples on plots for which there is any evidence of cultural or historical artifacts. These sites are coded as not sampled, and plot notes are recorded to explain why soil samples were not taken. A memorandum of understanding is currently in place to allow collection of samples of National Forest System lands. To obtain permission to sample on national parks and other Federal lands, FIA must present a research plan and apply for a permit.

8.3 Shipping, Storage, and Disposal of Pest-regulated Soils

To limit the movement of agricultural pests (e.g., fire ant, corn cyst nematode, golden nematode,

karnal bunt, witchweed, and Mexican fruit fly), the shipment of soil samples across State boundaries is strictly regulated by the Plant Protection and Quarantine program of the USDA Animal and Plant Health Inspection Service (APHIS). States with regulated pests are primarily located in the South, but other locations are restricted as well (fig. 14). Detailed information on APHIS quarantine regulations are available online (see http://www.aphis.usda.gov/ppq/permits/soil/).

To receive a permit to accept soil samples from these areas, FIA soil labs have signed compliance agreements with APHIS. These compliance agreements require that all soil samples be stored or disposed of in a prescribed manner. Labs must also pass an inspection before receiving their permit and are subject to unannounced inspections by regional APHIS officers. APHIS samples are clearly labeled as regulated soils throughout the analysis process and are sterilized before disposal. All packing materials that come into contact with regulated soils are incinerated.

Before sending samples to the lab, crews are required to double bag or enclose all samples inside of a larger plastic bag or other leak proof container. All shipments must be clearly identified as "Regulated Material," and a label containing the appropriate APHIS permit number must be attached to the outside of the box.

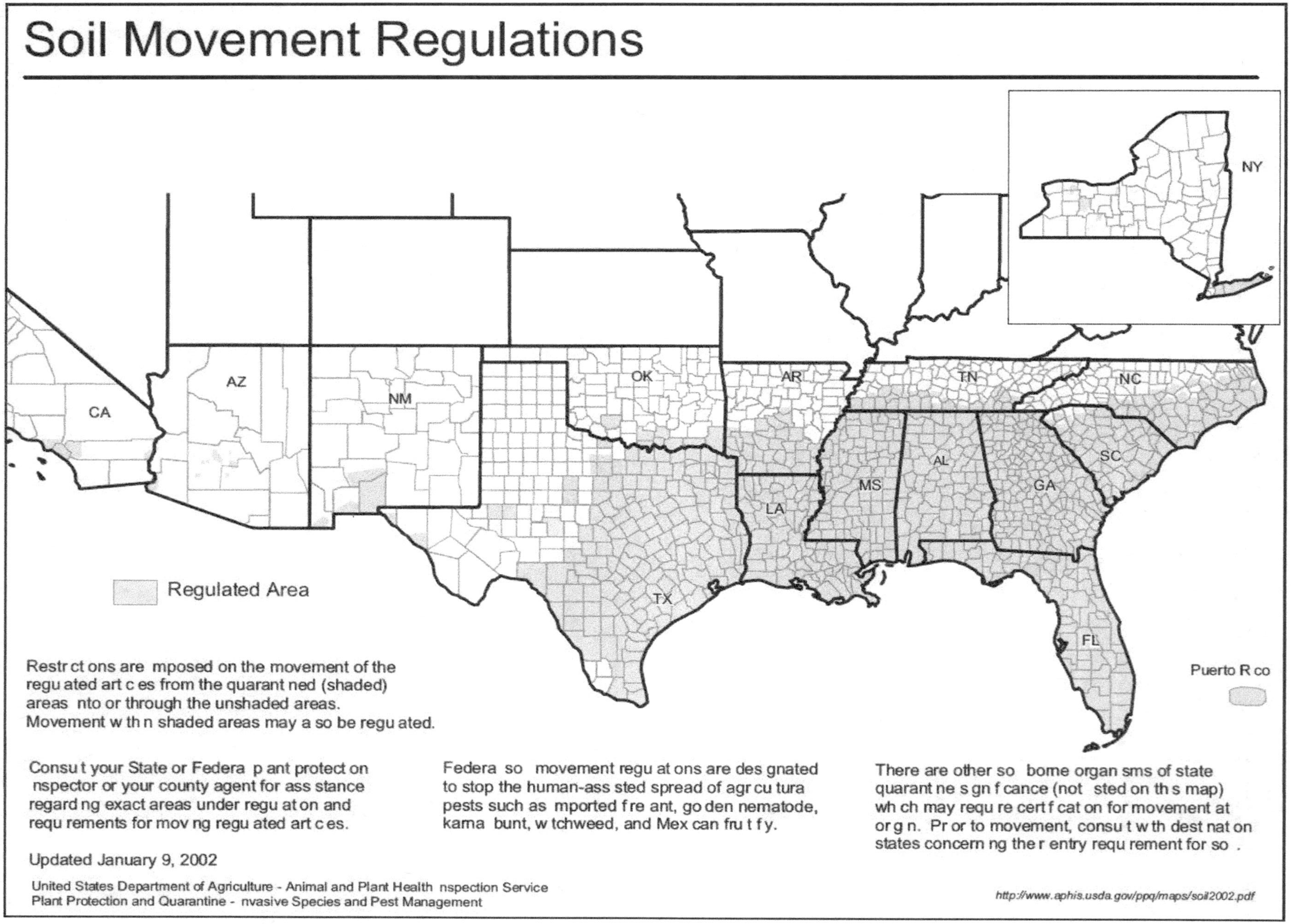

Soil Movement Regulations

Restrictions are imposed on the movement of the regulated articles from the quarantined (shaded) areas into or through the unshaded areas. Movement within shaded areas may also be regulated.

Consult your State or Federal plant protection inspector or your county agent for assistance regarding exact areas under regulation and requirements for moving regulated articles.

Federal soil movement regulations are designated to stop the human-assisted spread of agricultural pests such as imported fire ant, golden nematode, karnal bunt, witchweed, and Mexican fruit fly.

There are other soilborne organisms of state quarantine significance (not listed on this map) which may require certification for movement at origin. Prior to movement, consult with destination states concerning the reentry requirement for soil.

http://www.aphis.usda.gov/ppq/maps/soil2002.pdf

Updated January 9, 2002

United States Department of Agriculture - Animal and Plant Health Inspection Service
Plant Protection and Quarantine - Invasive Species and Pest Management

Regulated Area

NY

Puerto Rico

NC
SC
FL
GA
TN
AL
MS
AR
LA
OK
TX
NM
AZ
CA

Figure 14.—States and counties with soil movement restrictions. [Adapted from APHIS.]

9. SUMMARY

The FIA soil indicator program represents the only repeated, systematic sampling of key indicators of soil quality in all forested regions of the U.S. regardless of ownership. Integration of soil assessments within the larger framework of the national FIA program provides a mechanism for systematic monitoring of soil properties using nationally standardized collection, preparation, and data distribution formats that are fully compatible with existing forest inventory and forest health data (McRoberts *et al.* 2004). When fully implemented, the soil indicator program will provide critical information on the status of forest soils that can be used to meet regional, national, and international reporting requirements. Analysis of soil indicator data requires interpreting soil variables in the context of the larger landscape. Soil properties naturally vary as a function of factors such as climate, vegetation, topography, parent material (geology), and the age of the soil. As a result, it is often not possible to establish a threshold value for "good" and "bad" levels of a particular soil nutrient, erosion, or compaction level that will be valid across the entire country. The strength of the soil indicator lies in its ability to detect change over time. However, in the early years of implementation, the focus of the program must be on establishing baseline levels for soil variables. Additional research is still needed to determine appropriate baselines and thresholds for assessing forest health and linking plot measurements to the underlying processes regulating forest productivity and ecological function.

For more information on the soil indicator or for assistance with specific questions or analyses, please contact your regional FIA office (http://www.fia.fs.fed.us) or the authors of this report.

10 GLOSSARY

Unless stated otherwise, all definitions are from the Soil Science Society of America glossary, available online at: http://www.soils.org/sssagloss/.

Acidity, active
The activity of hydrogen ion in the aqueous phase of a soil expressed as a pH value.

Acidity, residual
Soil acidity that is neutralized by lime or a buffered salt solution to raise the pH to a specified value (usually 7.0 or 8.0) but that cannot be replaced by an unbuffered salt solution. It can be calculated by subtracting salt replaceable acidity from total acidity.

Acidity, exchangeable
The aluminum and hydrogen that can be replaced from an acid soil by an unbuffered salt solution such as KCl or NaCl.

Adsorption
The attraction of ions or compounds to the surface of a solid.

Anion
A negatively charged ion (e.g., PO_4^{3-}, NO_3^-).

Bulk density
The weight of dry soil per unit bulk volume. The value is expressed as grams per cubic centimeter ($g\ cm^{-3}$).

C:N ratio
The ratio of the weight of organic carbon to the weight of organic nitrogen in soil, organic material, plants, or microbial cells.

Cation
A positively charged ion (e.g., Na^+, Ca^{2+}).

Cation exchange capacity (CEC)
The sum of exchangeable bases plus total soil acidity at a specific pH value, usually 7.0 or 8.0. Expressed in centimoles of charge per kilogram of exchanger ($cmol_c\ kg^{-1}$).

Clay
(i) A soil separate consisting of particles <0.002 mm in equivalent diameter. (ii) A textural class. (iii) A naturally occurring material composed primarily of fine-grained minerals, which is generally plastic at appropriate water contents and will harden when dried or fired.

Coarse fragment content
In FIA, the gravimetric fraction of the bulk soil derived from particles larger than 2 mm in diameter.

Effective cation exchange capacity (ECEC)
When acidity is expressed as salt extractable acidity, the cation exchange capacity is called the effective cation exchange capacity (ECEC) because this is considered to be the CEC of the exchanger at the native pH value. Expressed in centimoles of charge per kilogram of exchanger ($cmol_c\ kg^{-1}$).

Erosion
The wearing away of the land surface by rain or irrigation water, wind, ice, or other natural or anthropogenic agents that abrade, detach, and remove geologic parent material or soil from one point on the earth's surface and deposit it elsewhere.

Exchangeable nutrient
A plant nutrient held by the adsorption complex of the soil and easily exchanged with the anion or cation of neutral salt solutions.

Litter
The surface layer of the forest floor that is not in an advanced stage of decomposition, usually consisting of freshly fallen leaves, needles, twigs, stems, bark, and fruits.

Mineral soil
A soil consisting predominantly of products derived from the weathering of rocks (e.g., sands, silts, and clays).

Nutrient
Elements or compounds essential as raw materials for organism growth and development.

O horizon
A layer of organic material that has undergone little or no decomposition (fibric material). On the forest floor this layer consists of freshly fallen leaves, needles, twigs, stems, bark, and fruits.

Organic soil

In FIA, any soil in which the organic horizon is greater than (20 cm) 8 inches in thickness. These soils are prevalent in wetland areas such as bogs and marshes and may be frequently encountered in certain regions (e.g., Maine, northern Minnesota, coastal regions).

pH

The acidity of a solution in equilibrium with soil. It is determined by means of an electrode or other indicator at a specified soil-solution ratio in a specified solution, usually distilled water, 0.01 M $CaCl_2$, or 1 M KCl.

Porosity

The volume of pores in a soil sample (nonsolid volume) divided by the bulk volume of the sample.

Restrictive layer

In FIA, any soil condition that increases soil density to the extent that it may limit root growth. This limitation may be physical (hard rock) or chemical (acid layer) or both.

Sampling frame

In FIA, a frame used to collect forest floor samples from a known area. A bicycle tire 12 inches in diameter has been selected as the national standard.

Soil profile

A vertical section of the soil through all its horizons and extending into the C horizon.

11. REFERENCES

Anonymous. 1995.
Sustaining the world's forests: the Santiago agreement. Journal of Forestry. 93: 18-21.

Amacher, M.C.; O'Neill, K.P. 2004.
Assessing soil compaction on Forest Inventory & Analysis Phase 3 field plots using a pocket penetrometer. Res. Pap. RMRS-RP-46WWW. Fort Collins, CO: U.S. Department of Agriculture, Forest Service, Rocky Mountain Research Station. 7 p.

Amacher, M.C.; O'Neill, K.P.;
Conkling, B.L. [In review].
Watershed Erosion Prediction Project (WEPP) soil erosion rates for Forest Inventory & Analysis (FIA)/Forest Health Monitoring (FHM) Phase 3 plots in Idaho. Gen. Tech. Rep. RMRS-XXX. Fort Collins, CO: U.S. Department of Agriculture, Forest Service, Rocky Mountain Research Station.

Amacher, M.C.; O'Neill, K.P.;
Dresbach, R.; Palmer, C.J. 2003.
Laboratory methods in the Forest Inventory and Analysis (FIA) soil indicator program. St. Paul, MN: U.S. Department of Agriculture, Forest Service, North Central Research Station. [Available online: www.ncrs.fs.fed.us/4801/national-programs/indicators/soils/analysis/] (accessed 5 November 2004).

Amacher, M.C.; Henderson,
R.E.; Breithaupt, M.D.; *et al.* 1990.
Unbuffered and buffered salt methods for exchangeable cations and effective cation-exchange capacity. Soil Science Society of America Journal. 54: 1036-1042.

Brady, N.C.; Weil, R.R. 1996.
The nature and properties of soil. 11th ed. Upper Saddle River, NJ: Prentice-Hall. 740 p.

Brand, G.J.; Nelson, M.D.;
Wendt, D.G.; Nimerfro, K.K. 2000.
The hexagon/panel system for selecting FIA plots under an annual inventory. In: McRoberts, R.E.; *et al.* eds. Proceedings, First annual Forest Inventory and Analysis symposium; 1999 November 2-3; San Antonio, TX. Gen. Tech. Rep. NC-213. St. Paul, MN: U.S. Department of Agriculture, Forest Service, North Central Research Station: 8-13.

Burger, J.A.; Kelting, D.L. 1999.
Using soil quality indicators to assess forest stand management. Forest Ecology and Management. 122: 155-166.

Conkling, B.L.; Coulston, J.W.;
Ambrose, M.J., eds. [In press].
2001 Forest Health Monitoring national technical report. Gen Tech. Rep. SRS-XXX. Asheville, NC: U.S. Department of Agriculture, Forest Service, Southern Research Station.

Dissmeyer, G.E.; Foster, G.R. 1981.
Estimating the cover management factor (C) in the universal soil loss equation for forest conditions. Journal of Soil and Water Conservation. 36(4): 235-240.

Dissmeyer, G.E.; Foster, G.R. 1984.
A guide for predicting sheet and rill erosion on forest land. Tech. Pub. R8-TP 6. Atlanta, GA: U.S. Department of Agriculture, Forest Service, Southern Region. 40 p.

Elliot, W.J.; Hall, D.E.; Scheele, D.L. 2000.
Disturbed WEPP: WEPP interface for disturbed forest and range runoff, erosion, and sediment delivery. Technical Documentation. Moscow, ID: U.S. Department of Agriculture, Forest Service, Rocky Mountain Research Station. [Available online: forest.moscowfsl.wsu.edu/fswepp/docs/distweppdoc.html] (accessed 5 November 2004).

Fisher, R.F.; Binkley, D. 2000.
Ecology and management of forest soils. 3d ed. New York: John Wiley. 489 p.

Foster, G.R.; Renard, K.G.;
Yoder, D.C.; *et al.* 1996.
RUSLE user's guide. Ankeny, IA: Soil and Water Conservation Society. 173 p.

Kuo, S. 1996.
Phosphorus. In: Sparks, D.L.; *et al.*, eds. Methods of soil analysis. Part 3. Chemical methods. Madison, WI: Soil Science Society of America: 869-919.

Kurtz, J.C.; Jackson, L.E.; Fisher, W.S. 2001.
Strategies for evaluating indicators based on
guidelines from the Environmental Protection
Agency's Office of Research and Development.
Ecological Indicators. 1: 49-60.

Lal, R.; Blum, W.H.;
Valentinin, C.; Stewart, B.A. 1997.
Methods for assessment of soil degradation.
Advances in soil science. Chelsea, MI: Lewis
Publishers. 558 p.

Marschner, H. 1986.
Mineral nutrition of higher plants. London:
Academic Press. 674 p.

McRoberts, R.E.; McWilliams,
W.H.; Reams, G.A.; *et al.* 2004.
Assessing sustainability using data from the
Forest Inventory and Analysis program of the
United States Forest Service. Journal of
Sustainable Forestry. 18 (1): 23-46.

Miles, P.D. 2002.
Using biological criteria and indicators to
address forest inventory data at the State level.
Forest Ecology and Management. 155: 171-185.

Nelson, D.W.; Sommers, L.E. 1996.
Total carbon, organic carbon, and organic matter.
In: Sparks, D.L.; *et al.*, eds. Methods of soil
analysis. Part 3. Chemical methods. Madison,
WI: Soil Science Society of America: 961-1010.

O'Neill, K.P.; Amacher, M.C. 2004.
Criterion 4. Conservation of soil and water
resources. Indicator 18: area and percent of
forestland with significant soil erosion. In:
National report on sustainable forests, 2003.
Rep. FS-766. Washington, DC: U.S. Department
of Agriculture, Forest Service: 32.

O'Neill, K.P.; Woodall, C.;
Amacher, M.C. 2004.
Cross-Indicator analysis: combining soil and
down woody material inventories to monitor
changes in carbon storage at the regional scale.
In: Forest science in practice: Proceedings,
Society of American Foresters 2003 national
convention; 2003 October 25-29; Buffalo, NY.
Bethesda, MD: Society of American Foresters:
102-110.

O'Neill, K.P.; Amacher,
M.C.; Palmer, C.J. [In press].
A national approach for monitoring physical and
chemical indicators of soil quality on U.S. forest-
lands as part of the Forest Inventory and
Analysis program. Environmental Monitoring
and Assessment.

O'Neill, K.P.; Woodall, C.;
Amacher, M.C. [In progress].
Assessment of carbon stocks in soil and downed
wood in forests of the North Central U.S. using
Forest Inventory and Analysis data. Forest
Ecology and Management.

Overton, W.S.; White, D.;
Stevens, D.L., Jr. 1990.
Environmental monitoring and assessment pro-
gram: design report. EPA/600/3-91/053.
Washington, DC: U.S. Environmental Protection
Agency, Environmental Monitoring and
Assessment Program. 52 p.

Potash and Phosphate Institute. 1995.
Soil fertility manual. 16th printing, revised.
Norcross, GA: Potash and Phosphate Institute.
116 p.

Renard, K.G.; Foster, G.R.;
Weesies, G.A.; Porter, J.P. 1991.
RUSLE: Revised Universal Soil Loss Equation.
Journal of Soil and Water Conservation. 46(1):
30-33.

Renard, K.G.; Foster, G.R.;
Weesies, G.A.; *et al.* 1997.
Predicting soil erosion by water: a guide to con-
servation planning with the Revised Universal
Soil Loss Equation (RUSLE). Agric. Handb. 703.
Washington, DC: U.S. Department of
Agriculture. 404 p.

Schlesinger, W.H. 1991.
Biogeochemistry: an analysis of global change.
San Diego, CA: Academic Press. 443 p.

Sherrod, L.A.; Dunn, G.;
Peterson, G.A.; Kolberg, R.L. 2002.
Inorganic carbon analysis by modified pressure
calcimeter method. Soil Science Society of
America Journal. 66: 299-305.

Smith, W.B. 2002.
Forest inventory and analysis: a national inventory and monitoring program. Environmental Pollution. 116: S233-S242.

Soil and Plant Analysis Council. 1999.
Soil analysis handbook of reference methods. Boca Raton, FL: CRC Press. 264 p.

Soil Survey Laboratory. 1996.
Soil survey laboratory methods manual. Soil Survey Invest. Rep. 42. Version 3.0. Lincoln, NE: U.S. Department of Agriculture, Natural Resources Conservation Service. 716 p.

Sparks, D.L. 1995.
Environmental soil chemistry. San Diego, CA: Academic Press. 267 p.

Stolte, K.; Conkling, B.;
Campbell, S.; Gillespie, A. 2002.
Forest health indicators, Forest Inventory and Analysis program. FS-746. Washington, DC: U.S. Department of Agriculture, Forest Service. 24 p.

Sumner, M.E.; Miller, W.P. 1996.
Cation exchange capacity and exchange coefficients. In: Sparks, D.L.; et al., eds. Methods of soil analysis. Part 3. Chemical methods. Madison, WI: Soil Science Society of America: 1201-1229.

Taiz, L.; Zeiger, E. 1991.
Plant physiology. Redwood City, CA: Benjamin/Cummings Publishing Co. 564 p.

Thomas, G.W. 1996.
Soil pH and soil acidity. In: Sparks, D.L.; et al., eds. Methods of soil analysis. Part 3. Chemical methods. Madison, WI: Soil Science Society of America: 475-490.

Tkacz, B.M. 2003.
Forest Health Monitoring. St. Paul, MN: U.S. Department of Agriculture, Forest Service, State and Private Forestry, Forest Health Protection. [Available online: http://fhm.fs.fed.us/fact/index.htm] (accessed 5 November 2004).

U.S. Department of Agriculture. 2000.
Summary report: 1997 National Resources Inventory (revised December 2000). Washington, DC: U.S. Department of Agriculture, Natural Resources Conservation Service: Ames, IA: Iowa State University, Statistical Laboratory. 89 p.

U.S. Environmental Protection Agency. 1997.
Environmental monitoring and assessment program (EMAP) research strategy. EPA/620/R-98/001. Washington, DC: U.S. Environmental Protection Agency, Office of Research and Development. 17 p.

Waring, R.H.; Schlesinger, W.H. 1985.
Forest ecosystems: concepts and management. San Diego, CA: Academic Press. 340 p.

White D.; Kimerling, A.J.;
Overton, W.S. 1992.
Cartographic and geometric components of a global sampling design for environmental monitoring. Cartography and Geographic Information Systems. 19: 5-22.

Wischmeier, W.H.; Smith, D.D. 1978.
Predicting rainfall erosion losses: a guide to conservation planning. Agric. Handb. 537. Washington, DC: U.S. Department of Agriculture. 58 p.

Woodall, C.W.; Williams, M.S. 2005.
Sampling protocol, estimation, and analysis procedures for the down woody materials indicator of the FIA program. Gen. Tech. Rep. NC-256. St. Paul, MN: U.S. Department of Agriculture, Forest Service, North Central Research Station. 47 p.

12. LIST OF FIGURES

13. LIST OF TABLES

www.ingramcontent.com/pod-product-compliance
Lightning Source LLC
Chambersburg PA
CBHW080547290526
45790CB00006B/2588